MAGNOLIAS, PORCHES & SWEET TEA

PAT BRANNING

MAGNOLIAS, PORCHES & SWEET TEA

RECIPES, STORIES & ART FROM THE LOWCOUNTRY

PAT BRANNING

Daffodil Field, watercolor on paper by Nancy Ricker Rhett.

PHOTOGRAPHER ANDREW BRANNING

Magnolias, Porches & Sweet Tea

Recipes, Stories & Art from the Lowcountry

Copyright © 2013 by Patricia Anderson Branning, original content only. All artwork copyright remains with artists. (3-CB)

Photography by Andrew Branning, Copyright © 2013.

All rights reserved. No portion of this book may be reproduced, stored in a retrieval system, or transmitted in any form or by any means mechanical, electronic, photocopying, recording, or otherwise-without prior written permission from the publisher, except as provided by United States of America copyright law.
Printed in China

International Standard Book Number, 978-0-9896340-0-7

Proofread by Lindsay Gifford.

Published by Andrew Branning Publishing, LLC. Please contact Publisher for wholesale information. (info@andrewbranning.com)

To order individual copies of this book please visit the author's website at www.patbranning.com.

Opposite Page;
Magnolias, Porches & Sweet Tea,
watercolor on paper by Nancy Ricker Rhett.

CONTENTS

ACKNOWLEDGMENTS 9

STARTERS Y'ALL 15
FROGMORE STEW ON A STICK 16
CRAB & CORN FRITTERS 17
HAM & PIMENTO CHEESE PARTY BISCUITS 18
ICED PINEAPPLE MINT TEA 19
OYSTERS ROCKEFELLER 20
OYSTERS BIENVILLE 22
STRAWBERRY SALAD 25
CAPRESE APPETIZER 26

SOUTHERN FARM VEGETABLES 28
GRANDPAPPY'S POKE SALLET 32
ARUGULA PESTO 33
MUSHROOM POLENTA STUFFED COLLARD GREENS 35
SQUASH GALETTE 36
BAKED SQUASH CASSEROLE 39
MAMA'S BUTTER BEAN & CORN SUCCOTASH 40
CAROLINA CORN PUDDING 41
ZIP'S SWEET POTATO SOUFFLÉ 44
FRIED GREEN TOMATO BLT PO BOYS 45

SMALL GRAINS, BIG FLAVOR 46
SOUTHERN BUTTERMILK CORNBREAD 50
HEIRLOOM GRAINS & GOLDEN FRUIT SALAD 53
GEECHIE BOY CREAMY GRITS 54
FABULOUS BAKED GRITS 56
CASHEW BROWN RICE SALAD 57
CHARLESTON SHRIMP PILAU 58
BROWN RICE MUFFINS 59

WHEN THE DINNER BELL RINGS 60
PAN-FRIED QUAIL & COUNTRY GRAVY 64
BILLY'S VENISON MEDALLIONS 65
DOVES WITH BACON CREAM SAUCE 66
MIDDLETON BAKED GUINEA HEN 70
MIDDLETON PLACE PORK BELLY & JOHNNY CAKES 71
FRENCH CHICKEN IN WHITE WINE SAUCE 74
HOLIDAY CHICKEN SALAD 75
BRAISED SHORT RIBS ON POLENTA 76
PEPPERCORN CRUSTED BEEF TENDERLOIN 77
PECAN CRUSTED PORK TENDERLOIN 78
SERIOUS SOUTHERN STROGANOFF 79

TREASURES OF THE SEA 80
SEARED AHI TUNA SALAD 85
SHRIMP, CRAB & BEAN SALAD 88
MUSSELS MARINIERE 91
SOFT SHELL CRAB 92
JAMBALAYA STRUDEL 94
CRAZY CRAB BENEDICT 95
BLACKENED MAHI ON TOMATO COULIS 98
AMEN STREET SHRIMP & GRITS 99

SPOONFULS OF COMFORT 101
VIC'S FRENCH ONION SOUP 102
SEA ISLAND SHRIMP BISQUE 103
SHE CRAB SOUP 105
CAROLINA BRUNSWICK STEW 107
ST. SIMONS CRAB STEW 108
BISQUE OF
WINTER SQUASH 111

THE SUMMER KITCHEN 113
SWEET CORN CHOW-CHOW 114
PLANTATION PICKLED OKRA 117
SWEET POTATO BUTTER 118
PEACH GINGER JAM 119
CHICKEN & WATERMELON SALAD 120
RUSTIC HEIRLOOM TOMATO SALAD 121
STRAWBERRY - RHUBARB JAM 122
SIMPLY SUMMER PEACH PIE 125
RASPBERRY CRUMP PIE WITH HOMEMADE PIE DOUGH 126
SAVANNAH GREEN TOMATO COBBLER 127

GRAND FINALES 129
CHOCOLATE FRUIT TART 130
FLOURLESS CHOCOLATE CAKE WITH GANACHE 131
PUMPKIN SPICE ICE CREAM PIE 132
CAROLINA GOLD RICE PUDDING 134
EDNA LEWIS' FRESH APPLE CAKE 135
FRESH STRAWBERRIES OVER CORN FLAKE RUSK 138

Opposite Page: Tools of the Trade, oil on canvas by Hilarie Lambert.

ACKNOWLEDGMENTS

Toast to the areas finest chefs who laid their recipe cards on the table and taught me how they put together fresh local seafood, produce, meats and products to create all forms of deliciousness. A heartfelt thank you to each and every incredible chef who was generous enough to allow me to eavesdrop. What a great pleasure to be invited into such distinguished Southern kitchens to linger awhile, taste and be inspired.

Now I pass that inspiration on to you and pair it first with some of the finest art from our beloved Lowcountry. May these lovely works lift your spirits as the recipes excite your appetites and generate an even greater appreciation and love for this magical place we affectionately call the Lowcountry. My special appreciation goes to Nancy Ricker Rhett, whose extraordinary work and talents grace the cover and many pages throughout this book.

And I must acknowledge my dear son, Andrew, who has traveled with me down southern roads these past two years, creating fine art photographs of people, places and all forms of culinary delights. Thank you, Andrew, for the courage to now tread fearlessly into the world of publishing.

Much praise to my husband, Cloide, and to my daughters Elizabeth & Margaret for their loving support. And a heartfelt thank you to my Dad (Carelton T. Anderson), without whom this work would not be possible.

The Hammock, oil on canvas by Joe Bowler.

WELCOME TO THE LAND OF MAGNOLIAS, PORCHES & SWEET TEA

No one can deny that Southerners know how to entertain! So gather 'round my big front porch as I serve you a tall glass of sweet tea and welcome you to this special place for all occasions. Anywhere South of the Mason-Dixon line, you just know our tea is sweet. Sweet tea is as basic to our way of life as our beloved magnolia trees. In fact, I think we could name it the "Sweet Tea Line."

Front porches have long been a way of life in the deep South, a vehicle for preservation of oral history, or socialization, a way to spread the news and perhaps a bit of gossip. It's here we gather after supper, sweet tea in hand and a plate heavy with Mama's Peach Cobbler.

The evening may start inside around the supper table but we always settle out on the front porch glider and the worn wicker rockers with the littlest ones climbing onto laps. Our yellow lab thumps his tail on the wooden floor in contentment, with one eye open to keep watch for visitors, as we tell tales and catch up on news from neighbors who happen by. Add soft summer breezes, the scent of freshly mowed grass and the cadence of our Southern orchestra of Whippoorwills, cicadas and bullfrogs, with someone strumming softly on an old banjo – *and that's summer in the South.*

This is where we laze in a swing for a nap with overhead fans turning slowly, chat with friends who stop by to refresh and revitalize. It's the part of the house that gives shade, serves as a conduit for breezes, shelter from rainstorms, and above all, a place to gather. *The porch is the heart and soul of the South.*

Our afternoon sweet tea is more than a refreshment, it's a ritual, probably a descendant of the proper British High Tea. It means it's time to sit a spell and cool off, or maybe just take a break. It's the liquid binder between friends and family, and the ice breaker between newly introduced strangers. It's almost medicinal in its importance.

And the banjo symbolizes our musical lives and our sense of place. Its sound can be melodic or poignant – jangly or raucous. It can be plucked or strummed. It can make you cry from nostalgia or clap and stamp your feet from joy. It's ubiquitous, found everywhere from a cabin to a mansion, from a wintertime oyster roast to a hot summer evening on the porch. *Yes, the banjo is the sound of the South.*

The idea of family is behind much of what defines my particular style of cooking. I want easy recipes that I can prepare in advance and when friends arrive at my door, the whole house smells wonderful and delicious.

Freshness and simplicity are key, so expect a lovely Caprese appetizer, as well as main courses with spanking clean tastes, such as Seared Ahi Tuna with Wasabi, Blackened Mahi, Mahi, and recipes that reflect our culinary heritage such as Braised Short Ribs with Creamy Polenta, and Carolina Gold Rice Pudding. Autumn Apple Cake pays homage to former chef-in-residence, Edna Lewis, of Charleston's Middleton Place. It's the farmers, fishermen, chefs and caterers who have left their marks on our food culture and inspired me to continue to write about this magical place we affectionately call the Lowcountry.

So curl up on a front porch rocker or settle into your favorite chair and sit a spell, relax with a tall glass of sweet tea and enjoy the journey into the Southern kitchens of some of our areas finest chefs & artists.

View our beloved South through the eyes of Lowcountry artists and start yearning to cook, gather with friends, swap stories and enjoy some real Southern cuisine.

Ace Basin, oil on canvas by Jennifer Smith Rogers.

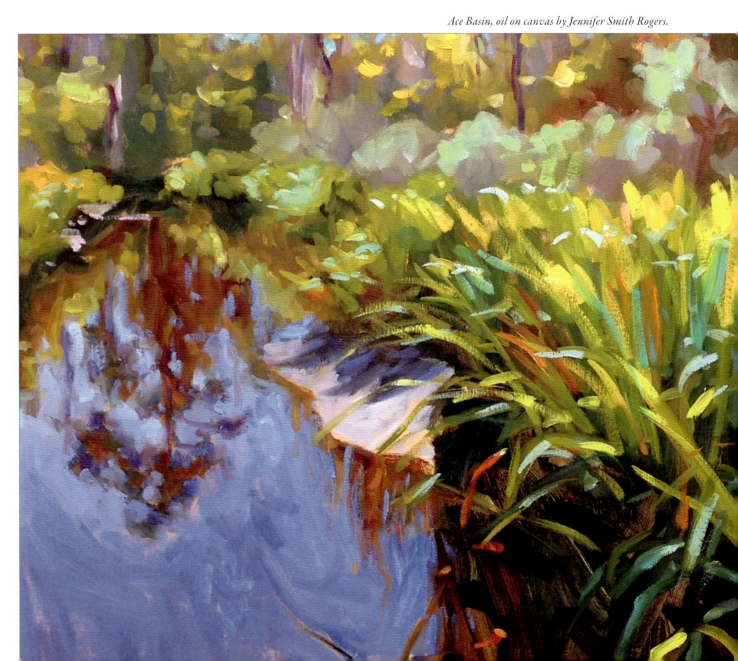

STARTERS Y'ALL

More often than not, entertaining in the South is casual–a sunset barbecue, a picnic under the shade of a centuries old live oak, a boating expedition or a dockside potluck. But with the arrival of the PGA players each spring, entertaining on Hilton Head Island goes to a whole new level. Each April, the island comes alive with festivities in celebration of the Heritage Golf Tournament held in Harbor Town.

FROGMORE STEW ON A STICK

SERVES: 7

Inspired by Chef Kevin Cavanaugh of the South Carolina Yacht Club.

These delicious skewers were served at Hilton Head Island's first "Palate to Palette" party where artists from Charleston presented their artwork while guests strolled through the displays enjoying some of our finest Lowcountry cuisine. It was an evening that will be long remembered.

St. Helena Island near Beaufort used to have a town center called Frogmore, named after an ancestral English country estate. This is where the stew originated.

1. Preheat oven to 350°. In a large bowl, sprinkle shrimp with pepper, salt and red pepper flakes. Drizzle oil over the shrimp and toss to coat. Spread shrimp evenly on a baking sheet. Roast in oven for about 10 minutes until fully cooked. Shrimp will be opaque. Set aside.

2. Quarter potatoes evenly, cover with cold water. Bring water to a boil, reduce heat and simmer several minutes until potatoes are tender but not mushy. Pat dry and fry in batches until lightly browned on all sides. Remove from skillet onto a paper towel lined plate. Set aside.

3. Cut casing off the andouille sausage and slice into 1/2 inch cubes. Spread on a greased baking sheet and roast in oven for 10 minutes until crispy. Remove and set aside on paper towels.

4. To assemble skewers: first place potato, sausage, shrimp, corn and then tomato. Repeat. Serve with Fire Roasted Cocktail Sauce.

Previous Page: Opening Ceremony, oil on canvas by Jim Palmer.

INGREDIENTS

24 shrimp
24 pieces of red new potatoes
24 andouille sausage cubes
24 pieces Asian mini corn, *cut into 1/4 inch pieces*
24 sun-dried tomatoes, *steeped in hot water*
24 skewers or bamboo knot picks (4inches)

SHRIMP

peel and devein shrimp
1 tablespoon freshly ground black pepper
1 tablespoon Kosher salt
1/2 cup extra virgin olive oil
pinch of ground red pepper flakes

FIRE ROASTED COCKTAIL SAUCE

1/2 cup fire roasted tomatoes, *blend if chunky*
4 tablespoons horseradish sauce
1/2 cup ketchup
1/2 teaspoon Worcestershire sauce
1 teaspoon lemon juice
salt and pepper to taste
Whisk together

Pullin the Pots, watercolor on paper by Nancy Ricker Rhett.

CRAB & CORN FRITTERS

SERVES: 8-10

Inspired by Chef Kevin Cavanaugh of the South Carolina Yacht Club.

INGREDIENTS

1/2 pound jumbo lump crab meat
2 ears of sweet corn, *oven roasted*
1/2 cup small diced red bell pepper
1/2 cup small diced red onion
1 tablespoon minced garlic
2 tablespoons chopped fine parsley
1 tablespoon extra virgin olive oil

FRITTER BATTER

1 cup all-purpose flour
1/2 cup coarse purified wheat flour
1 cup milk
1 egg, *lightly whisked*
Salt and freshly ground black pepper

1. Heat oil in a heavy bottomed skillet, over medium-high heat. Add onion and bell pepper. Cook for 3 minutes until translucent. Add garlic and parsley, cook for 1 minute. Remove from heat. Drain liquids. Let cool.

2. In a large mixing bowl, combine batter, onion mixture, crab meat and corn. Heat 3 tablespoons canola oil in a heavy bottomed skillet over medium heat. Carefully spoon batter into skillet, using spoon to shape batter into small cakes. Cook through and brown fritters on each side. Remove from skillet and place on paper towel lined plate.

HAM & PIMENTO CHEESE PARTY BISCUITS
YIELDS: 24 BISCUITS

The treasured historic demeanor of our coastal towns and villages take on a special glow at holiday time with doorways garlanded with our own island inspired decorations. Locals tend to gather together with friends and neighbors to enjoy the camaraderie experienced this time of the year.

A relaxed style of entertaining featuring lovely finger foods that can be made ahead and put together quickly when guests drop by is the order of the day.

These little biscuits are a savory splurge, sure to have friends leaving with visions of sugarplums. Enjoy them at holiday time or anytime.

INGREDIENTS
2 cups sharp grated cheese
1/2 cup Duke's mayonnaise
1/2 cup pimentos, *drained*
1/4 cup green onion, *chopped fine*
1 teaspoon freshly ground black pepper
1/2 teaspoon salt
1/4 teaspoon cayenne
dash of Tabasco
Thoroughly combine all ingredients and store in the refrigerator until ready to use.

BISCUIT
2 cups all-purpose flour
4 teaspoons baking powder
3 teaspoons sugar
1/2 teaspoon salt
1/2 cup milk
1 egg
1 tablespoon honey

1 BISCUIT, In a bowl combine the flour, sugar, baking powder and salt. Cut in shortening until the mixture resembles course crumbs. Combine egg, milk, and honey and stir in flour until just combined. Turn onto floured surface and knead. Roll out and cut with a very small biscuit cutter 1/2 inch thick. Bake at 425° about 10 minutes until golden brown.

2 Spread pimento cheese on your favorite little round biscuits, top with a piece of baked ham, then refrigerate until ready to serve.

Heron, watercolor by Kathy Crowther.

Tea Time, oil on canvas by Walt Gonske.

ICED PINEAPPLE MINT TEA

YIELDS: 12 SERVINGS

Fruity but not too sweet. This drink is a favorite of students in Chef Darin's Lowcountry cooking classes at Savannah's 700 Kitchen at the Mansion on Forsyth. My daughter, Margaret, and I enjoy spending time in Chef Darin Sehnert's Lowcountry kitchen. He is a delight and we never go away without plenty of new inspiration.

INGREDIENTS

1 quart water
1 cup sugar
5 spearmint tea bags
1 quart cold water
1 quart pineapple juice

1. In a large 4 quart pan combine water and sugar. Place on the stove over high heat and bring to a boil. Stir to help dissolve sugar and then turn off the heat and add the tea bags. Let it steep and infuse for at least 30 minutes. Remove tea bags, squeezing gently. Stir in cold water and pineapple juice. Refrigerate until well chilled. Serve over ice and garnish with fresh mint leaves.

OYSTERS ROCKEFELLER
SERVES: 6-8

INGREDIENTS

2 dozen oysters on the half shell
4 tablespoons unsalted butter
2 garlic cloves, *minced*
1/3 cup Panko bread crumbs
2 shallots, *chopped fine*
6 tablespoons fresh spinach, *finely chopped*
1 tablespoon Pernod
salt and freshly ground black pepper
2 tablespoons olive oil
1/4 cup grated Parmesan
3 tablespoons chopped parsley
Tabasco to taste
rock salt
lemon wedges, *for garnish*

This dish was given the name Rockefeller because the green is the color of greenbacks and the whole dish is extremely rich. According to legend, it was a customer at Antoine's restaurant in New Orleans who exclaimed with delight after eating this dish, "Why, this is as rich as Rockefeller!"

1. Using an oyster knife, pry open the oyster shells and remove oysters. Discard the top shells; scrub and dry the bottom shells. Drain oysters and reserve the oyster liquor.

2. In a large saucepan, melt the butter; add spinach, shallots, parsley, bread crumbs, Tabasco sauce, Pernod and salt. Cook, stirring constantly, for 15 minutes. Remove from heat. Press the spinach mixture through a sieve or food mill. Let cool.

3. Place an oyster in each shell and add a little of the reserved oyster liquor on each oyster. Spoon an equal amount of the prepared spinach mixture over each oyster and spread to the rim of the shell.

4. Broil about 5 minutes or until the edges of the oysters have curled and the topping is bubbling.

5. Garnish the plates with parsley and lemon wedges. Serve at once.

Tony Gray of the Bluffton Oyster Factory.

OYSTERS BIENVILLE
SERVES: 6

Originally created at Antoine's Restaurant in New Orleans, the flavors and aromas of scallions, garlic and bacon bring back cherished memories of dining in some of the finest restaurants from Charleston to Savannah. Oysters from the salt-misted shores of the Lowcountry are among the finest in the world.

The Lowcountry contains one of the most extensive systems of salt marsh and tidal flats in the country. Each day, the two high tides inundate this vast area of the coast, maintaining a system of channels, creeks and rivers where oysters thrive as they are washed by the nearly 8 foot tides.

1. Use a large heavy bottomed skillet to fry the bacon until crispy. Add the onions, salt and cayenne and cook, stirring, for several minutes. Add the garlic and butter and continue to cook and stir until the butter melts. Add the flour, stirring slowly and constantly, cooking for 2 more minutes. Add the milk, and Vermouth and stir to blend. Reduce the heat to medium, and add the mushrooms and parmesan cheese. Mix and blend until the mixture cooks and become very thick, about 10 minutes. Add the lemon juice, scallions, and parsley and stir to mix well. Remove from the heat, add the yolks, and blend well. Let it cool.

2. Preheat oven to 400°. Take out a large baking sheet and place oyster shells on a bed of rock salt. Put an oyster in each shell and top it with about 2 heaping tablespoons of the sauce. Bake until the sauce is browned and the oysters just begin to curl on the edges.

INGREDIENTS

1/2 pound sliced bacon, *chopped*
1 cup onions, *chopped*
1/2 stick unsalted butter
1 teaspoon salt
1/2 teaspoon cayenne pepper
2 teaspoon chopped garlic
1 cup flour
1/4 cup parmesan cheese
2 cups whole milk
1/2 cup dry Vermouth
2 cups mushrooms, *trimmed and sliced*
3 tablespoons lemon juice
1/2 cup chopped scallions, *green part only*
3 tablespoons chopped parsley
4 egg yolks, *lightly beaten*
3 dozen oysters, *shucked, drained and bottom shells reserved*
rock salt

Opposite Page: Sunset Boulevard, oil on canvas by Joseph Orr.

STRAWBERRY SALAD
SERVES: 6

This table setting is at the home of well-loved Charleston artist, Betty Anglin Smith. Betty loves to collect vintage tablecloths and napkins. Her charming home and studio overlooks Wadmalaw Sound.

Betty is the mother of triplets – each one an artist. Her work and that of her daughters, Jennifer Smith Rogers and Shannon Smith Hughes, are presented throughout this book

INGREDIENTS
6 cups baby spinach leaves
2 cups strawberries, *hulled and quartered*
1/4 cup toasted pecans
1/2 cup feta cheese
2 tablespoons balsamic vinegar

VINAIGRETTE
1/4 cup rice vinegar
2 tablespoons sugar
2 teaspoons poppy seeds
1/2 teaspoon dry mustard
salt and freshly ground black pepper
3/4 cup grape-seed oil

1. Take out a heavy bottomed frying pan and toast the pecans over medium heat, stirring until they start to brown, about 5 minutes. Cool and coarsely chop. Set aside.

2. For the vinaigrette, whisk together the rice, vinegar, sugar, poppy seeds, dry mustard, and a little salt and pepper. Add the oil whisking constantly until well blended.

3. Toss the spinach, strawberries, feta cheese and pecans into a salad bowl. Add some vinaigrette and toss gently.

4. Briefly marinate the strawberries in the balsamic vinegar to enrich their flavor. Toss with spinach and pecans into the salad bowl. Add some vinaigrette and toss gently.

CAPRESE APPETIZER
YIELDS: 24

Sultry summer days call for light, healthy, simple appetizers that can be put together in a matter of minutes. Your guests will love these tasty skewers with all the elements of a classic caprese salad. Make these in advance if you like, but be sure to let them come to room temperature before serving – much more flavorful that way.

Tomatoes are truly summertime's superstars and these little bite-size ones brighten up the platter and are so delicious with fresh basil.

INGREDIENTS
24 grape tomatoes
24 cherry-size fresh mozzarella cheese balls, *drained*
24 fresh basil leaves
1 jar marinated artichoke hearts
1 package sun dried tomatoes
1/4 teaspoon thyme
a sprinkling of Kosher salt
freshly ground black pepper

1. Soak the package of sun dried tomatoes in warm water until soft. Drain the water and continue to soften in olive oil and thyme. Drain oil from the sun dried tomatoes after about 20 minutes.

2. Drain oil from the packaged mozzarella balls and begin to assemble on little skewers. Alternate the vegetables on the skewers for a beautiful presentation. Once assembled sprinkle with Kosher salt and freshly ground black pepper. Voilá! You are ready to serve and enjoy.

Opposite Page: Garden Bouquet, oil on canvas by Dan McCaw.

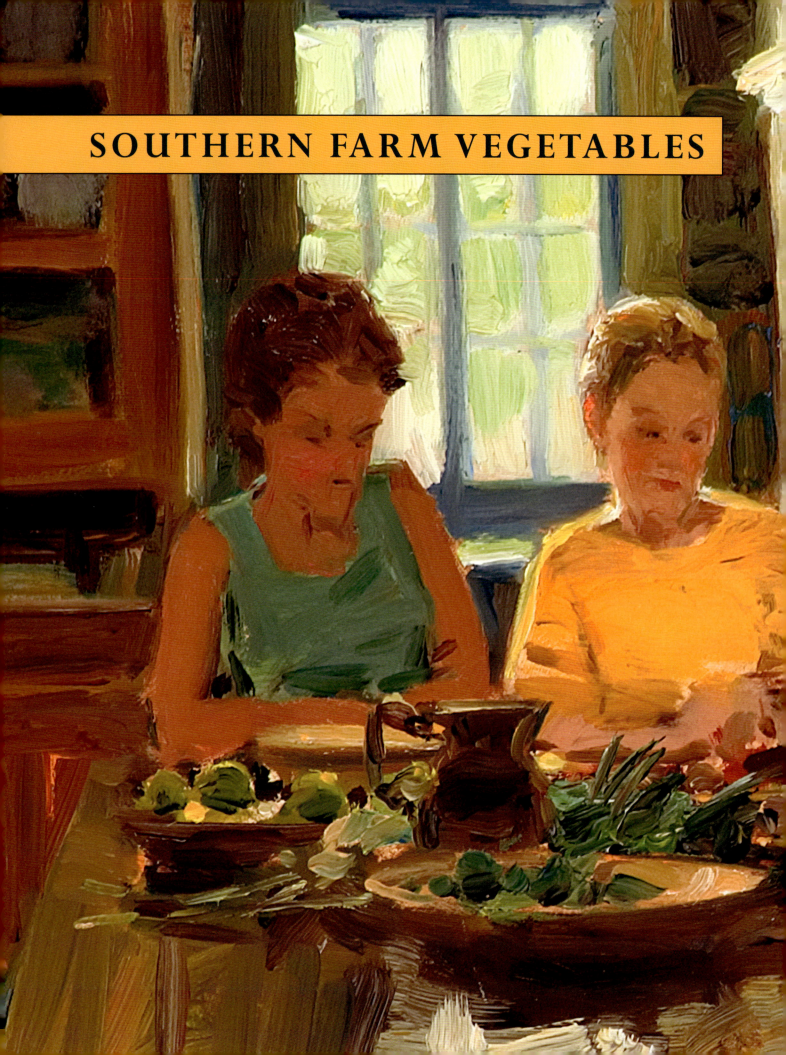

SOUTHERN FARM VEGETABLES

Another Sunny Day, oil on canvas by Kathleen Dunphy.

LOCAL, FAST & FRESH

I think I have always grown something to eat whether it was an avocado seed in a glass jam jar, lettuce along a strip of my mother's garden, or okra climbing up a trellis in a big clay pot on my apartment balcony in Atlanta. I've always had a curiosity about vegetables that extends beyond all other ingredients.

Farmer's markets beckon me to come out and shop among the tomatoes and lettuces. The beauty of garden lettuce reminds me of the cottage garden roses I grew on our land in North Carolina. I like to take time to browse the assorted tomatoes in hues of scarlet, orange, yellow and green. But more than that I like to grow heirloom tomatoes, watching green shoots poke through the soil, and looking after them like precious children, watering and weeding and getting the rich, dark soil of the good earth under my finger nails. It's an experience that awakens the senses with a pull back to what is basic and real.

The beauty of this vegetable patch is loaded with even greater sensual pleasure once I reach the kitchen. I love a summer supper of sweet and creamy squash casserole, watermelon and feta salad over red leaf lettuce, crisp cucumber refrigerator pickles, a sauté of green beans with roasted red peppers, and best of all a generous plate of sliced sun-ripened garden fresh tomatoes. None of this is difficult, time-consuming, or expensive and the benefits of a largely plant based diet go beyond taste.

When you peak into my stockpots on the stove or lift the lid of my casseroles, it's the veggies that play the starring role. Our food production in this country has become so filled with pesticides, ways of extending shelf life, packaging and marketing, that I yearn for something simpler and more satisfying.

Previous Page: Cooking Lessons, oil on canvas by David Hettinger.

GRANDPAPPY'S POKE SALLET

SERVES: 4

Golden Beets, oil on canvas by Nancy Hoerter.

In the American South, there's a particular reverence for a "mess of greens." I'm talking about collard, mustard and turnip greens mainly, but old timers would add poke weed.

For country folk all across the South, this lovely wild green miracle of spring is a genuine piece of Southern lore. Just so you understand, the term sallet means cooked greens and salad means uncooked. This harbinger of spring known as poke weed is likely to turn up under your magnolia tree in the backyard or in the shade of the azalea bushes around back.

The root and berries are poisonous but the first shoots that grow in the spring are a great delicacy. They are green to reddish purple in color. Once the stalk and leaf stems become a little red, the season for gathering them is over.

1 Gather tender shoots when about 4 inches tall. Pick and wash greens in water at least 3 times. Discard water after each washing.

2 Trim off the tough stems and bring them to a boil in a large pot. Once wilted, drain and rinse under cold water. Remove any excess liquid.

3 Place bacon pieces into a skillet and fry until browned and crispy. Spoon onto paper towels leaving a couple tablespoons of fat in the pan.

4 Add the onion and sauté until translucent. Add the greens to the pan and cook for about 5 more minutes. Bring the pepper vinegar to a boil along with the salt and cayenne pepper. Pour pepper vinegar over chilies and seal.

5 To serve top with bacon bits and pass around the Pepper Vinegar.

INGREDIENTS

2 pounds tender sallet leaves
4 slices thick sliced bacon cut into pieces
1 large onion, *peeled and chopped*
Kosher salt and freshly ground black pepper

PEPPER VINEGAR

6 ounces fresh red or green hot chilies, *place chiles into a jar*
1 1/2 cups cider vinegar
1/4 teaspoon salt
a pinch of cayenne pepper

ARUGULA PESTO
YIELDS: 1 1/2 CUPS

The popularity of arugula originated in Italy, but I've found it grows like wildfire in my garden and will reseed itself when there is no hard winter freeze. It's wonderful to discover creative ways of using its peppery goodness. It makes a delicious base for pizza in place of marinara, dresses up grilled chicken and fish and makes a wonderful sandwich spread.

1. Combine the arugula, parsley, almonds or pine nuts, lemon juice, and garlic in the bowl of a food processor fitted with a metal blade. Pulse several times until a paste forms, stopping several times to scrape down the sides of the bowl.

2. Slowly add the olive oil with the processor running. Once the mixture is smooth, add the Asiago, salt and pepper and pulse until well combined. Keep in the refrigerator until ready to use.

INGREDIENTS

5 cups packed arugula, *washed, drained and stems removed*
1/2 cup parsley
1/2 cup toasted pine nuts or almonds
juice of 1 lemon
1 head of garlic cloves, *minced*
1/2 cup virgin olive oil
1/2 cup Asiago cheese, *shredded*
Kosher salt and freshly ground black pepper

Market Day, oil on canvas by Kim English.

Farm vegetables have come to symbolize for me the essence of what it means to live in and love the South; baskets of cascading leafy lettuce on rickety farm stands, watermelons fresh from the soil, sweet summer cantaloupes, earthy tasting fresh-dug sweet potatoes from our salt misted shores and our beloved shell peas. Southerners cherish lady peas, crowders, zippers, pink-eyes and butter beans.

Sweet Grass Basket, oil on canvas by John Carroll Doyle.

MUSHROOM POLENTA STUFFED COLLARD GREENS

SERVES: 6

Inspired by Ambrose Farms on Wadmalaw Island, SC.

Did you know that collard greens are prehistoric? Ancient Greeks and Romans grew them. They came here from West Africa where they were eaten for centuries before they were brought to North America by slaves. Today, collards, along with mustard and turnip greens, are a staple at African-American meals and celebrations. Collard greens are great leaves to stuff. Simply remove the stems, blanch them, fill, and cook. It was at Oak Plantation, St. Helena Island, that I met Chef Sherri whose cooking is rooted in love and family tradition.

INGREDIENTS

1 fresh bunch of collards, *stem cut and blanched (6-8)*
1 cup polenta, *precooked according to the directions on the bag*
1 tablespoon olive oil
1/2 cup fresh mushrooms, *chopped*
1 shallot, *chopped*
1 garlic clove, *minced*
1 teaspoon fresh thyme, *chopped*
1/4 cup parmesan cheese
2-3 cups tomato or bolognese sauce

TOMATO SAUCE

1/4 cup olive oil
1 onion, finely diced
1 bay leaf
1 teaspoon chopped fresh oregano
2 cloves minced garlic
2 teaspoons sea salt
2 tablespoons tomato paste
2 (28 ounce) cans whole plum tomatoes, chopped

1. Preheat oven to 350°. Heat olive oil in pan and add mushrooms, shallots, garlic and sauté 5 minutes. Cook polenta, add parmesan and mushroom-shallot mixture along with the thyme. Cool polenta. Scoop onto collard leaves and roll up. Place all in casserole and cover with sauce and bake 35-45 minutes.

2. TOMATO SAUCE, Heat oil in a pan and add onions, bay leaf, oregano, garlic, salt and pepper. Cook about 10 minutes and add the tomato paste. Add tomatoes and stir until it begins to boil. Lower heat and simmer for 1 hour.

Chef Sherri Whitmire of Bonnie Hall Plantation.

SQUASH GALETTE
SERVES: 2-4

Inspired by Chef Robert Wysong of Colleton River.

Starting in June, squash becomes plentiful in the Lowcountry so you'll need to have a lot of different ways to serve this hearty vegetable. Here's a wonderful dish I learned while visiting Chef Robert's grand southern kitchen at Colleton River Plantation.

INGREDIENTS
1 medium zucchini, *sliced*
1 medium yellow squash, *sliced*
1 small eggplant, *peeled and sliced*
1 tomato, *quartered*
1 red onion, *peeled and quartered*

PARSLEY OIL
1 bunch Italian parsley, *washed, stemmed and roughly chopped*
3 garlic cloves, *peeled*
1 cup olive oil

1. PARSLEY OIL, Blend all together in a blender until a bright green oil forms. Reserve.

2. Lightly brush sliced zucchini, yellow squash and eggplant tomato and onion with parsley oil and season to taste.

3. Broil until tender and lightly caramelized. Allow to cool and serve on a platter garnished with the roasted tomato and onion.

BAKED SQUASH CASSEROLE
SERVES: 2-4

Inspired by Chef Robert Wysong of Colleton River.

Chefs Kitchen, oil on canvas by Shannon Smith Hughes.

Raised to be southern in mid-Atlantic Maryland, Robert now calls the coastal Lowcountry home. He found his place where southern culture and customs meet cuisine, climate, and environment. A graduate of Johnson & Wales in Charleston, he is now a lifetime student of cooking and hospitality.

Following the philosophy of social customs in agreement with nature, this restaurateur, hotelier, teacher and chef now calls upon the full breadth of his experience to guide the team of culinary and dining professionals in their unique private golf club setting.

1 Slice squash then blanche, refresh and drain.

2 Peel and slice the shallot, shred aged Gouda, and warm cream. Slowly add 1/2 of the Gouda cheese, reserving remaining for topping.

3 Arrange squash and shallot in an oven-proof baking dish. Season vegetables, and add fortified cream and cheese mixture.

4 Bake at 350° for 20 minutes until creamy and bubbly. Remove from oven and add remaining Gouda. Dust with Panko.

5 Bake another 10 minutes until nicely browned. Cool slightly and serve.

INGREDIENTS
1 medium zucchini, *sliced*
1 medium yellow squash, *sliced*
1 small shallot, *peeled and sliced*
1 cup heavy cream
1 cup dry aged Gouda, *finely shredded*
1 tablespoon Panko
salt and pepper

Blue Bottles, oil on canvas by Hilarie Lambert.

MAMA'S BUTTER BEAN & CORN SUCCOTASH
SERVES: 2-4

You can't get more Southern than succotash. This recipe comes from my North Carolina born and raised mother, who was a wonderful cook. This dish made her famous – at least with everyone who ever tasted it.

Summertime is when our Lowcountry markets are full of fresh beans, green and speckled butter beans, pink-eyes, zipper peas, pink-eyes – the beloved peas of the South!

1. In a heavy cast iron skillet sweat the onion and garlic in olive oil until the onion is translucent. Add the okra, butter beans, corn, tomatoes, bell pepper and chicken stock.

2. Turn down the heat and simmer for about 1 hour or until the vegetables are tender. Stir in the basil just before serving.

INGREDIENTS

1 onion, *finely chopped*
4 cloves garlic, *finely chopped*
6 tablespoons olive oil
1 cup sliced okra
2 cups fresh or frozen butter beans
2 cups grilled corn kernels
1 (28 ounce) can whole tomatoes
1 red bell pepper, *chopped*
2 cups chicken stock
2 tablespoons fresh basil chiffonade

CAROLINA CORN PUDDING

SERVES: 6-8

Perfectly sweet and pearly white silver queen kernels make their debut every year in late June and July. Surely trumpets should sound with the arrival of this most beloved vegetable. Saw the kernels off the cob, and sprinkle them over a salad of fresh greens or combine them with lima beans and smoked sausage for succotash. Better yet, try them in this creamy corn pudding.

1. ROASTED RED PEPPER SAUCE. Roast peppers either in the oven or over a gas flame on the stovetop. To roast in the oven: cover them with olive oil and place the whole pepper on a baking sheet in a preheated 450° oven. Turn it until the skin is charred on all sides, about 20 minutes. Once cooled, remove the charred skin, stem, core and seeds, leaving as much flesh as possible. To roast over a gas flame, use tongs and hold the peppers, one at a time, over a high flame, rotating the pepper until all sides and charred. Combine in a processor with rest of ingredients.

2. Preheat oven to 350°. Butter a deep 3 quart casserole dish. Combine corn, scallions, red bell pepper, cornmeal, sugar, basil, salt and pepper in a large bowl and stir to combine.

3. Whisk the half and half and eggs together in a separate bowl and stir in the cheese. Combine the egg mixture with the corn mixture.

4. Bake for approximately 1 hour or until nicely browned. Remove from the oven and let it come to room temperature before serving. Serve with warm Roasted Pepper Sauce.

INGREDIENTS

1 tablespoon unsalted butter
1 1/2 cups fresh or frozen corn
2 scallions, *trimmed and minced*
1/2 red bell pepper, *cored, seeded, and diced*
1 tablespoon yellow cornmeal
2 tablespoons sugar
2 teaspoons chopped fresh basil
2 teaspoons salt
1 teaspoon freshly ground black pepper
1 cup half and half
5 large eggs, *beaten*
1 cup grated cheddar cheese
1 cup Roasted Red Pepper Sauce

ROASTED RED PEPPER SAUCE

2 roasted red bell pepper, *peeled, cored and seeded*
4 garlic cloves, *minced*
8 basil leaves
1/4 cup olive oil
1 tablespoon white wine vinegar
1 tablespoon lemon juice
salt and freshly ground black pepper

VIDALIA'S ON MY MIND

Savannah's Monterey Square, oil on canvas by Walt Gonske.

One of the surest signs of spring in Georgia arrives each year with a sweet crunch – and a promise not to make your eyes water. The Vidalia onion season is officially open and the state's growers are shipping the first batches of sweet bulbs to anxious retailers everywhere.

Seeing them on store shelves, I'm all of a sudden 24 years old again, living on the Beaufort River at the far end of Lady's Island during the 1970s. I hadn't lived there long before a neighbor from Lucy Creek, Mr. Ed, came by and asked if I wanted to be put on the Vidalia onion list. As I was standing on the porch, he called out to me from the cab of his pickup truck, his tanned forearm resting on the open window. A ruggedly handsome man, he spent his days working out in the tomato fields by his house, and hunting quail and wild turkey.

"What kind of onion?" I asked. "An onion you can eat like an apple," he replied. "Really?" I wasn't sure it was up my alley, regardless of how eager I was as a newcomer to put my finger on the pulse of what makes those south of the Mason Dixon line different from those in the rest of the nation. I admit it. I was a little skeptical. "Never heard of 'em," I said.

With that he got out of the truck, reached around into the flat bed and pulled a large onion out of a twenty pound burlap sack. The bags in the back were all marked with names ready for delivery. Taking a pocket knife out of the front pocket of his bib overalls, he peeled back the skin, then took a bite. I'd never seen anything like it. There were no tears coming down his cheeks and he wasn't even making a face.

"Sign me up," I said. It's hard for most of us to remember a time when those sweet Georgia-grown Vidalias were available only across the border deep in the heart of Georgia. But that was the way it was in the years before they caught on and reached their current star status.

So each year, Mr. Ed took onion orders from friends across town, got in his rusted Chevy pickup truck and despite the 3 hour drive, made the pilgrimage several times each spring to pack up enough onions to last through the summer months, on into the fall and, if stored properly, on through Christmas. Keep in mind that gas prices were running around 35 cents a gallon in the 1970's. Not too many folks remember that either.

Just how would I store twenty pounds of onions? One thing for sure, if I needed to find out about anything in Beaufort, lunch at Harry's restaurant on Bay Street was the fastest way. As I was soon to discover, even casual conversations would more than likely get into something about those Vidalia onions coming to town.

"Save all your old pantyhose," I was told. "Onions must be stored in the legs of old, clean pantyhose. Tie a knot between each onion, and cut the knot when ready to use one. They'll keep better if they never touch. Then be sure to hang them in a cool, dry, well ventilated area." And that was a universal practice amongst onion enthusiasts throughout the Lowcountry on up to Augusta, Columbia and Atlanta. Walk into just about anyone's basement and you would find dozens of pairs of pantyhose hanging from the ceiling filled with those delicious sweet Vidalias.

Georgia became so proud of its famous treat that in 1990 they made it their official state vegetable. Vidalias boast their own cuddly mascot, the Yumion, and even have a festival in their honor and a museum. Their sweetness has made them a treasured ingredient in recipes from salads to muffins, homemade onion rings, relishes and even cookies. First cultivated and sold in the east central section of the Peach State, they're grown in loamy soil low in sulfur. Sulfur is the key – it's the mineral that gives rotten eggs their trademark stench and traditional onions their edgy bite that makes you cry.

Unlike many produce items, we can trace the origin of these sweet onions. What is now a deeply-entrenched summer tradition started out as a fluke. In the spring of 1931, Mose Coleman discovered that the onions he planted on his farm in Toombs county were not hot, as he expected – they were sweet! He apologized for them at first, but it didn't take long after people began tasting them for this sweet onion to become a "hot" commodity!

Often referred to as Coleman's sweet "gold mine" other farmers in the area began planting the onion seed in the sandy soil of South Georgia to sell to an ever-growing group of consumers. Soon the farmer's market built in Vidalia experienced a thriving tourist business. As fortune would have it, a Piggly Wiggly grocery store happened to be headquartered in Vidalia. Recognizing the potential, the gentleman who ran "The Pig" gladly helped farmers from all over the area get their newfound sweeties on store shelves.

There's more to the humble onion than you might think – today it's as synonymous with the South as sweet tea, pimento cheese and watermelon slices.

Having difficulty finding Vidalias at your local market? Just order a fresh batch along with salad dressings, salsas and other products at www.vidaliavalley.com.

Blackeyed Susans, oil on canvas by Joe Bowler.

ZIP'S SWEET POTATO SOUFFLÉ

SERVES: 8-10

The Five String Banjo, oil on canvas by John Carroll Doyle.

Cover artist Nancy Ricker Rhett is an original in every sense of the word and a true Renaissance woman. While she enjoys hunting, she is just at home in the kitchen cooking wild game and her famous sweet potato soufflé from her mother's recipe. She is a self-made artist, historian, avid birder, world traveler and consummate Southern lady.

Although I have lived here for many years, to view her paintings is to see the Lowcountry as if for the very first time.

Nancy grew up in Gardens Corner, located between Charleston and Beaufort, where her parents owned the Gardens Corner Motel and Restaurant – a restaurant recommended by *Gourmet* magazine. Nancy says, "Mother, whose name was Elizabeth was nicknamed, 'Zip' because Daddy's little brother couldn't pronounce her name. So he called her 'Lithazip' instead. She was a superb cook who hated to cook! Nonetheless, she did on occasion, and this is one of her most popular recipes." One word of caution: make plenty because people who don't even like sweet potatoes will come back for seconds!

INGREDIENTS

3 large cans sweet potatoes, *mashed*
1/2 teaspoon salt
2 large eggs, *beaten*
3/4 stick of butter
1/2 cup whole milk
1 teaspoon pure vanilla extract
1/2 teaspoon nutmeg
1/2 teaspoon cinnamon
a dash of sherry
lemon zest and lemon juice to taste

TOPPING

1 cup brown sugar, packed
1/3 cup flour
1 cup chopped pecans
1/2 stick butter, melted

1 Using a mixer, combine all the ingredients for the souffle. Spread evenly in a 9 x 11 pan.

2 In a bowl, combine ingredients for the topping and spread on top of the casserole.

3 Bake at 350° for 30 minutes until nicely browned.

Gullah Basket, oil on canvas by Nancy Ricker Rhett.

FRIED GREEN TOMATO BLT PO BOYS

SERVES: 4

Old Town Bluffton has maintained its reputation as a sleepy village with its own unigue charm and friendly people. Although development raged around it in recent years, the friendly folks along Calhoun Street have an authenticity not often found any more. After a couple visits shop owners greet you by name and ask how you're doing. Pathways around Calhoun make walking easy and there are more art galleries, shops, and restaurants than I can visit in an afternoon. Never do I leave there that I don't promise myself, "I'll be back soon."

Since the May River Grill has forever been a favorite of mine, I made an appointment with Chef/Owner, Charlie Sternburgh, to find out exactly how he makes his famous Fried Green Tomatoes. He graciously invited me to come out and cook fried green tomatoes with him and fix those ever popular salads. I could hardly wait to get there because if anyone knows how to make fried green tomatoes, it's Charlie.

1. Set up 3 bowls, one with white flour, one with beaten eggs and a third with panko crumbs.

2. Dip the tomato slices, one at a time into the flour, next the beaten eggs, and finally the panko crumbs. Press the panko slightly into the tomato so that each slice is fully coated.

3. Add The tomato slices to the hot oil in the pan on the stovetop, and being careful not to crowd the pan, put each piece into the oil and fry until golden brown, about 3 to 5 minutes per side. Turn them only once.

4. Remove each slice from the pan onto a paper towel lined surface and sprinkle with kosher salt.

5. Cover the inside of each baguette with Remoulade Sauce and place several slices of fried green tomatoes on the bread, followed by two bacon slices per roll, 1/2 sliced avocado per roll, and about 1/2 cup shredded lettuce per baguette.

INGREDIENTS

2 french bagettes
2 cups shredded lettuce
8 slices bacon, *fried crisp*
2 avocados
2 large green tomatoes

REMOULADE SAUCE

1/4 cup fresh lemon juice
3/4 cup canola oil
1 cup Vidalia onion, *finely chopped*
1/4 cup celery, *finely chopped*
2 cloves garlic, *minced*
2 tablespoons prepared horseradish
3 tablespoons whole-grain mustard
3 tablespoons yellow mustard
3 tablespoons chili sauce
3 tablespoons parsley, *finely chopped*
1 teaspoon salt
a pinch of cayenne pepper
freshly ground black pepper

SMALL GRAINS, BIG FLAVOR

Carolina Gold Rice was the basis of the colonial and antebellum economy in the Carolinas and Georgia, making Charleston the wealthiest city in the nation prior to the Civil War.

Sorghum, oil on canvas by Shannon Smith Hughes.

Carolina Gold is a medium-grain white non-aromatic rice with a subtle taste, hinting of hazelnuts, but its most distinctive trait is its wholesome mouth feel, and lusciously rich and nutty taste. Today, thanks to the work of Glenn Roberts, founder of Anson Mills, many of our heirloom grains are experiencing a revival. In 2000, Glenn had his first real harvest of Carolina Gold rice, as well as other varieties of Southern corns. He is the one who started milling grits for chefs throughout Georgia and the Carolinas and the circle has been widening ever since.

Rice built the tidewater regions of South Carolina, North Carolina and Georgia. Introduced to the colonies in the late seventeenth century, it provided enormous wealth to the plantation owners whose vast estates still define much of the Lowcountry landscape.

Rice growers clamored for slaves from Africa's coast and this influx of forced labor increased the population of plantations and quickly the black population outnumbered the white. And in turn, rice sowed the seeds of our definitive Southern cuisine - rice and greens, rice bread, rice pudding, hoppin' john and more.

Previous Page: Rice Fields, oil on canvas by William Rhett III.

Opposite Page: Bowl of Lemons, oil on canvas by John Carroll Doyle.

SOUTHERN BUTTERMILK CORNBREAD
SERVES: 6-8

"Cornbread is a hearty, rustic, humble Southern tradition."
Chef Frank Stitt of Birmingham's famed restaurant, Bottega.

Cornbread is as close to religion in the South as any one particular food gets, except perhaps barbecue. Like most of the South's beloved dishes, cornbread has roots that run deep, all the way back to the Native Americans who dried and ground corn into cornmeal. Their cornbread was simple, just cornmeal and water cooked on hot flat rocks in the fire and often called ash cake.

Around our dinner table we enjoy our cornbread with plenty of rich, luxurious sorghum syrup. Out in the fields of South Carolina, sorghum looks like a tall, wispy grain. However, the juice inside is pure culinary gold. It's what I remember putting on pancakes and warm buttered biscuits and cornbread when I was growing up. Both my parents were products of the deep South, so sorghum was a staple always found in our fridge. Just stick a spoon in the jar and drizzle away on waffles and toast or bake it into beans, barbecue sauce and cookies, creating a wonderful earthy sweetness without the dark sultry quality of molasses.

It's purer than molasses and more Southern than maple syrup – a more nostalgic alternative to honey or agave. And now it's becoming a pretty hot ingredient with all the attention paid to revitalizing foods from our past. It can be substituted cup for cup in any recipe that calls for molasses, honey, corn syrup or maple syrup. Try subbing it for molasses when making sweet potato pie.

Sorghum is sometimes called "Guinea grass" and came to this area with the slaves from West Africa, where it is indigenous. Both sugarcane and sorghum stalks are cut in the fall, ground and boiled and skimmed until the syrup is pure and of the just the right consistency.

INGREDIENTS
2 cups self-rising yellow cornmeal
1/2 cup all-purpose flour
3/4 cup whole milk
3/4 cup buttermilk
scant 1/2 cup rendered bacon fat
1 extra-large egg, *lightly beaten*

1. Preheat the oven to 450°.

2. Take out a large bowl and place the cornmeal and flour into it and stir. Add the whole milk and buttermilk a little at a time, mixing with a large wooden spoon.

3. Add the bacon fat to the preheated skillet, return to the oven and heat until the fat is very hot, about 5 minutes.

4. Remove the skillet from the oven. Pour the hot fat into the cornmeal mixture and stir to combine. Add the egg and stir gently until thoroughly combined. Pour the cornmeal mixture into the hot skillet and place it in the oven. Bake for 20 to 25 minutes until nicely browned. Serve with a dollop of luxurious sorghum.

HEIRLOOM GRAINS & GOLDEN FRUIT SALAD

SERVES: 6-8

Oranges, Too!, oil on canvas by John Carroll Doyle.

INGREDIENTS

1 cup cooked barley
1 cup cooked bulgur wheat
1 cup cooked orzo
6 ounces Garbanzo beans, *canned, rinsed and drained*
2 Valencia Oranges, *peeled and segmented in their own juice*
2 ounces golden raisins, *re-hydrated in orange juice or water*
2 ounces dried apricots, *sliced*
1 ounce shallots, *peeled and finely minced*
1/2 cup Italian parsley, *washed, stemmed, minced*
1/2 cup cilantro, *washed, stemmed, minced with some whole leaves reserved*

DRESSING

1 tablespoon extra virgin olive oil
1 tablespoon sherry vinegar
1 tablespoon honey
salt and pepper to taste
Whisk together

Here's what's cooking at Colleton River Plantation in Bluffton, S.C. Executive Chef Robert Wysong developed this special recipe for the members. He changes it up a bit according to the seasons but it is always as delicious as it is nutritious.

Recently I spent an afternoon in Robert's Southern kitchen at Colleton River Plantation where he created this sumptuous salad. What an inspiration to spend time with one of the best!

1. Cook barley and bulgur according to package directions. Drain and allow to cool. Cook orzo according to package directions. Drain and allow to cool.

2. Drain garbanzo beans. Peel and section oranges. Reserve juice.

3. Rehydrate golden raisins in juice or water and drain.

4. Slice dried apricots.

5. Combine cooked grains, pasta and beans. Add all fruit, shallots and herbs and combine. Add the dressing and toss. Chill before serving. Garnish with whole parsley and cilantro.

GEECHIE BOY CREAMY GRITS
SERVES: 6-8

Now's the time for puttin' on the grits. In a place where grits are practically a religion, it's not easy to impress. When some of Charleston's finest chefs began raving about the grits coming from a small farm in Edisto, I couldn't help but go for a drive and find out first hand.

Edisto Island is a flat, subtropical barrier island just south of Charleston. Most of the land is a jungle of oak trees tangled in Spanish moss, magnolia trees, palmettos, and yuccas standing high above a woodland floor. Great white and blue herons and pelicans populate the sky high above the tidal creeks and marshlands that meander through the forests. Alligators roam in search of prey while whippoorwills and cicadas create music as the sun goes down.

Approaching the island on Hwy. 174, Geechie Boy Market and Mill is situated on the right side of the road. The grits are the work of Greg Johnsman who takes a decidedly old-fashioned approach. Inside the rustic wooden store is an old gristmill where each batch of corn is ground daily, ensuring optimal freshness and flavor that has chefs so excited.

When cooking grits, I believe the secret to flavorful creamy grits is to use a combination of chicken stock and half and half or cream and cook very slowly over low heat for an extended period of time. The flavorful liquids add so much more than water alone. Long, low heat during the cooking process allows the grits to bloom, absorbing the liquid and swelling up instead of the liquid just simply evaporating from the pot. Once you have eaten freshly ground whole grain grits, the bland instant store-bought grits will never taste good again.

INGREDIENTS
1 1/2 cups stone-ground grits
3 cups chicken stock
3 cups milk
Kosher salt
freshly ground black pepper
4-5 tablespoons butter
1/2 cup parmesan cheese
1/4 cup half and half or heavy cream
Hot sauce, *optional*

1. Place chicken stock and milk in a large stockpot. Season with Kosher salt and black pepper. Add grits to the liquid and let it sit for about 15 minutes to begin hydration. Turn the heat to medium high and bring to a simmer. Once liquid simmers, reduce heat to very low and continue to cook, whisking once in awhile, for about 1 hour. At this time the liquid will be mostly absorbed and the grits will have lost their gritty texture and be soft and creamy. If consistency gets too thick you can always add more stock.

2. Stir in the butter, Parmesan cheese and heavy cream or half and half. Adjust seasonings to taste and serve warm.

Nothin' but a Hound Dog, oil on canvas by John Carroll Doyle.

FABULOUS BAKED GRITS
SERVES: 10

Use small molds for the grits cakes, then turn the mold upside down onto a plate after baking and cover with the warm Parmigiano-Reggiano sauce. This makes a wonderful side dish to your menu. You'll find these delicious little cakes make a tasty foundation for fresh fish dishes. Just bake or grill your fish and serve over baked grits.

1. In a large saucepan, bring the water and the salt to a boil, stirring with a wooden spoon. Add the grits in a slow, steady stream, stirring on a low temperature until thickened for about 1 hour. Remove pan from the heat and add the butter, Parmigiano-Reggiano and pepper, stirring until combined. Add the egg and stir to incorporate. Preheat the oven to 375° and butter ten 4-6 ounce molds.

2. Divide the grits among the buttered molds, place in a baking pan, and add enough hot water to the pan to come halfway up the sides of the molds. Cover with foil and bake for 15 minutes. Remove the foil and bake for about 20 minutes longer or until the tops are crusty and beginning to brown.

3. PARMIGIANA-REGGIANO SAUCE, In a medium sauté pan, combine the Vermouth, sherry, vinegar, shallots, bay leaf, and prosciutto and bring to a boil. Cook until only 1 tablespoon of liquid remains. Reduce the heat to low and stir in the cream. Whisk in the butter gradually.

4. Strain the sauce into a saucepan. Add the Parmigiana-Reggiano and season with salt and pepper and lemon juice and keep warm.

5. GARNISH, Heat olive oil in a small sauté pan over medium high heat. Add the julienned prosciutto, mushrooms and shallots and cook until the mushrooms are barely tender. Carefully unmold the grits onto serving plates and turn browned side up. Ladle a little sauce around the grits and top with the mushrooms and prosciutto. Garnish with thyme leaves.

INGREDIENTS
4 cups water
1 teaspoon Kosher salt
1 cup stone-ground grits
2 tablespoons unsalted butter
1/4 cup grated Parmigiana-Reggiano
freshly ground pepper to taste
1 large egg, *beaten*

PARMIGIANA-REGGIANO SAUCE
1/2 cup Vermouth
1/4 cup sherry vinegar, *to taste*
2 shallots, *minced*
1 bay leaf
2 ounces prosciutto
1 tablespoon heavy cream
8 tablespoons unsalted butter, *cut into cubes*
2 tablespoons finely grated Parmigiana-Reggiano
Kosher salt and freshly ground black pepper
Juice of 1/2 lemon, or to taste

GARNISH
1 tablespoon olive oil
2 thin slices prosciutto, cut into julienne strips
1/2 cup chanterelle mushrooms cut into 1 inch pieces
2 shallots, minced
thyme leaves for garnish

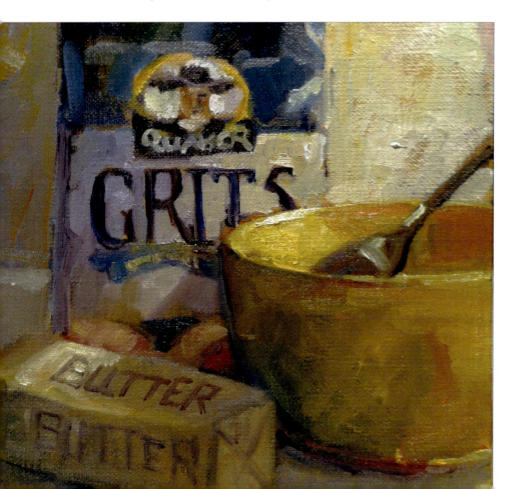

Grits, oil on canvas by Hilarie Lambert.

Quiet Southern Street, oil on canvas by Marilyn Simandle.

CASHEW BROWN RICE SALAD

SERVES: 2

Have served this salad many times over the years – always simple and delicious. Brown rice simply means it's hulled but not stripped of bran layers. Brown basmati has the same nutty aroma as white, with more chew and most brown short-grains cook just like white rice.

I adore this salad and regularly prepare it for picnics on the beach. When fall comes around, it's always at hit at tailgate parties by the stadium.

1. In a large bowl, combine the cooked rice, chopped red onion, golden raisins, curry, garbanzo beans and cashew nuts.

2. Mix all salad ingredients together throughly and pour the dressing over the top. Gently stir until well combined.

INGREDIENTS

2 cups cooked brown rice
1/2 cup red onion, *chopped*
1/2 cup golden raisins
1 teaspoon curry
1 1/2 cup garbanzo beans
1/4 cup cashew nuts

Dressing

1/2 cup canola oil
1/8 cup rice vinegar
1 clove garlic, *minced*
1 teaspoon honey mustard
Kosher salt and freshly ground black pepper

SMALL GRAINS, BIG FLAVOR

Backmans, oil on canvas by Mark Horton.

CHARLESTON SHRIMP PILAU
SERVES: 6

Without a doubt Pilau is the Lowcountry's most authentic and sacred signature dish originating from African slaves. Nothing defines us better than a single grain of Charleston Gold rice, surely the centerpiece of every Southern table.

1. Fry bacon until crispy and drain on paper towels. Crumble and set aside.

2. Cook rice according to package directions, adding bacon drippings to the cooking water.

3. In a heavy skillet, melt the butter and add oil to sauté the celery and bell pepper until tender.

4. Drizzle shrimp with Worcestershire then toss with flour. Add them to the skillet mixture and simmer for 5 minutes. Season with salt and pepper.

5. Add cooked rice and mix until well combined. Add more butter, if desired and stir in the crumbled bacon.

INGREDIENTS

5 slices bacon
1 cup Carolina Gold rice
2 tablespoons butter
1 tablespoon vegetable oil
1/2 cup celery, *chopped*
2 cups shrimp, *cleaned and deveined*
1/4 cup bell pepper, *chopped*
salt and freshly ground black pepper
1 teaspoon Worcestershire
1 tablespoon flour

BROWN RICE MUFFINS
YIELDS: 12 MUFFINS

Summertime just lends itself to a natural spontaneity as we go about our daily lives. With endless warming rays of sunshine to absorb, crested ocean waves to jump, and romantic novels to escape into, there is little time to plan menus in any traditional way.

These nutrient packed muffins are the perfect snack to pack in your lunch to nibble on at whim as you breeze through these lazy summer days - and don't forget the homemade jam!

INGREDIENTS
1 cup cooked short grain brown rice
1 1/4 cups sifted rice flour
2 teaspoons baking powder
1/2 teaspoon salt
1 cup whole milk
2 large eggs, *beaten*
4 tablespoons melted butter

1. Sift together the flour, baking powder, salt and sugar.

2. Combine the milk, eggs, butter and rice.

3. Quickly combine the two mixtures being careful not to over beat. Pour into 12 buttered muffin tins.

4. Bake in a 425° oven for 20 to 25 minutes, or until lightly browned.

In the Breeze, oil on canvas by Hilarie Lambert.

WHEN THE DINNER BELL RINGS

Dove, oil on canvas by William Means Rhett, Jr.

When the dinner bell rings in homes across the South, it's often time to gather the family round the table, serve some tall glasses of iced tea, plenty of steaming hot vegetables and good conversation. It's the end of the day when we pause to sit a spell and catch up on news of each other.

Delicacies such as dove, quail, venison, marsh hen and duck are served often and southerners learn to enjoy wild game from an early age. One thing for sure, no life on our sea islands is complete without at least one quail or dove shoot.

Southern boys may love their barbecue, steaks and fried chicken but they also love their hunting dogs, fishing, shooting and whiskey sipping. From the earliest days, native Americans taught settlers to this region how to hunt wild game, fish, and gather honey and oysters.

"To describe our growing up in the Lowcountry of South Carolina, I would have to take you to the marsh on a spring day, flush the great blue heron from its silent occupation, scatter marsh hens as we sink to our knees in mud, open an oyster with a pocketknife, and feed it to you from the shell and say, 'There. Taste that. That's the taste of my childhood.' - Pat Conroy, **The Prince of Tides**

Opposite Page: After the Hunt, oil on canvas by William Means Rhett, Jr.

Previous Page: Game-bag, oil on canvas by William Means Rhett, Jr..

Quail Hunt, oil on canvas by William Means Rhett, Jr.

PAN-FRIED QUAIL & COUNTRY GRAVY
SERVES: 4

When quail, champagne and cream come together in a pan, it's a winning combination! Avid hunters throughout the South serve this on a bed of grits for breakfast with savory cream gravy or with buttermilk mashed potatoes at supper time. Just be sure to watch out for a little bit of bird shot that may have been left behind!

1. Combine the Worcestershire, milk, minced garlic, salt and pepper in a large zip-lock bag or large mixing bowl. Place the quail in the bag or bowl and cover completely. Let marinate for an hour. Drain and pat dry.

2. Heat 1 tablespoon oil and butter in a large cast-iron skillet.

3. Using a small mixing bowl, combine the flour with the paprika, and thyme. One at a time, dredge the quail in the flour, shaking to remove any excess. Reserve the excess flour.

4. Fry in batches until golden brown and cooked thoroughly, turning once, 3-4 minutes per side. Remove and drain on paper towels and place them in a 200° oven to keep them warm.

5. For the milk gravy: deglaze the pan with the wine or champagne. Scrape up any bits from the bottom of the pan. Add the onions to the iron skillet and cook, over medium-high heat, until soft. Add 1 1/2 tablespoons of the remaining flour and cook, stirring, for 2 minutes. Add the cream and simmer, stirring continually, until thickened, 5-6 minutes. Add the chopped green onions, and parsley and cook for 1 minute.

6. Serve with mashed potatoes topped with 2 quail covered with gravy.

INGREDIENTS

8 whole quail, boneless, *rinsed and patted dry*
1 cup whole milk
1 tablespoon Worcestershire sauce
1 tablespoon garlic, *minced*
Kosher salt and freshly ground black pepper
2 tablespoons paprika
1 teaspoon thyme
1 tablespoon vegetable oil
4 tablespoons butter
3 cups all-purpose flour
1 cup champagne or dry white wine
1 large sweet onion, *chopped*
1 cup heavy cream
2 tablespoons chopped green onions
3 tablespoons chopped parsley

BILLY'S VENISON MEDALLIONS

SERVES: 4

Stag, oil on canvas by Nancy Ricker Rhett.

INGREDIENTS
1 venison tenderloin
1 small onion, chopped
1/4 teaspoon garlic powder
kosher salt and freshly ground black pepper
2 glugs red wine *(1 for the cook)*
1 package rice noodles

ROUX
1 cup butter
1 cup all-purpose flour
1 cup cream

1. Slice the tenderloin of well-processed venison into small medallions, no more than 1/2 inch thick. Sprinkle with garlic powder, salt and pepper.

2. Brown quickly on both sides in olive oil in a heavy skillet. Remove from pan.

3. ROUX, A roux is a thickener for sauces and soups that combines equal parts flour and butter. Begin by melting 1 cup butter in a saucepan over medium heat. Once hot, whisk in 1 cup flour gradually until a thick paste is formed. As it cooks the roux will become smooth and begin to thin.

4. After about 5 minutes of cooking and stirring, slowly add 1 cup cream to the roux while whisking and continue cooking to desired thickness. Cooking for about 35 minute will produce a sharp nutty taste.

5. Put the medallions into the roux, add the chopped onion and red wine and simmer, covered for 3 to 4 hours, adding liquid if needed. Serve over rice noodles.

Hunter, artist, acclaimed woodworker, historian and philosopher, Billy Rhett (William Means Rhett, Jr.) is a man of considerable talent, sharp wit and strong opinions. His wood sculptures of waterfowl are done feather by feather with the most meticulous eye for detail. Billy studied under Gilbert Maggioni, the Lowcountry icon, raconteur, artist, duck hunter and third generation oysterman. Billy Rhett was smitten and took on work at the oyster house just to study with Maggioni after hours. There was another aspiring carver on the docks named Grainger McCoy. Together they learned to take bird-carving from folk art to fine art.

Step into his kitchen on Lady's Island and you'll find among his many talents is cooking wild game. This is a prize venison recipe and he has a few recommendations about processing.

Venison must be hung in a cold locker just above freezing for 4 or 5 days, otherwise it has a very "gamey" taste which can be unpleasant. Properly cured, it's delicious. If you want to remove this game taste yourself, clean and divide meat into sections. Place in an ice chest, covered with ice. Change the melted ice water every day until there is no pink color to the water, usually 4 or 5 days. Cook venison either very quickly or very slowly. Anything in between and it's shoe leather!

DOVES WITH BACON CREAM SAUCE
SERVES: 4

INGREDIENTS
6-8 doves
12 slices of good bacon
3 egg yolks
1 1/2 cups heavy cream
1 teaspoon sweet Hungarian paprika
Kosher salt and freshly ground black pepper

1. Skin and clean doves.

2. In a large skillet, sauté the bacon until crispy. Drain on paper towels.

3. Using the same skillet sauté the birds on all sides over medium heat in the bacon fat. Salt and pepper to taste. Pour off all the fats except for about 3 tablespoons.

4. Beat the egg yolks with the cream. Add the 3 tablespoons of reserved fat. Pour the cream, egg and fat mixture back into the skillet and cook over low heat just to thicken. Stir constantly, but do not allow the mixture to boil.

5. Stir in the paprika and serve the sauce in a gravy dish.

6. Use the crisp bacon for garnish and enjoy with some stone ground grits or mashed potatoes.

Turkey Crossing, oil on canvas by William Means Rhett, Jr..

MIDDLETON PLACE PLANTATION
CHARLESTON, SC

History is the evolving story of people, places and events. But, if no one is paying attention, history can slip away and be lost forever.

Middleton Place is a National Historic Landmark just outside Charleston, the birthplace of one of the signers of the Declaration of Independence, one of the most significant rice plantations prior to the Civil War and a place that has remained under the same family stewardship for over 272 years.

The introduction of slavery into South Carolina laid the foundation for the lifestyle at Middleton Place that would anchor her way of life for generations.

On a recent visit to Middleton, it was the Plantation Stable-yards that captured my imagination. For this represents where African-American slaves cared for the animals and performed agriculture-related chores. Interpretive craftspeople demonstrate the work that would have been done by slaves on the plantations, who were extremely skilled and made tools, pottery, clothing and products to support a fully functioning plantation.

Jeff Neale of Middleton Place.

Many of the same breeds of water buffalo, sheep, goats and Guinea hens documented to have been at Middleton Place over the past two centuries, can still be seen there today. We visited the blacksmith working the bellows and anvil and watched Gulf Coast sheep being sheared in the grass nearby. Within the Stable-yards, a weaver, and a carpenter were also at work demonstrating their skills.

While the restaurant was founded in 1928, it was Edna Lewis, the granddaughter of freed slaves, who was to forever change the culinary landscape at Middleton Place when she became chef-in-residence in the late 1980's.

She became the caretaker of genuine Southern cooking. Her 1976 cookbook, *A Taste of Country Cooking* is a memoir of her childhood years growing up in Freetown, Virginia where her family lived close to the land. She went on to become the chef at Café Nicholson in New York City, a private chef to prominent New York families, a proprietor of a New Jersey pheasant farm and a teacher in the African Hall of the Museum of Natural History.

It was during her later years that she arrived at Middleton Place where her mission was to develop recipes for the historic plantation's restaurant. Today she is a legend whose influence lives on throughout the kitchens and gardens.

Today, Chef Brandon Buck carries forth many of her traditions and offers up an exceptional food experience for visitors by serving many of Edna Lewis' Southern staples. He invited us to taste his Heritage Farms Pork Belly and Guinea Hen the day I was there. Be sure to visit the dessert chapter and get The Middleton Place recipe for Banana Pudding. I've never had better, creamier banana pudding topped off with homemade vanilla wafers. There's an experience here like none other.

Ron Vido of Middleton Place.

Spring Flowers, oil on canvas by Peter Rolfe.

MIDDLETON BAKED GUINEA HEN

SERVES: 4

This deeply flavored fowl is one most American's have never tasted. We just can't drop by our local market and pick one up for dinner. Normally they are found at specialty markets by a few new-wave butcher shops that feature heritage breeds. However, this experience is available for those fortunate enough to dine at Middleton Place.

Chef Brandon Buck served us one in a cast iron pan that was positively delicious. It resembles pheasant, but juicier, and since the guinea is dark meat, the flesh really delivers flavor.

Less than an hour in the oven will give you a burnished, fragrant roasted hen.

INGREDIENTS

4 guinea hen breasts
1 bunch thyme
1 cup unsalted butter, *cut into cubes*
Kosher salt and freshly ground black pepper

1. Preheat oven to 350°. With a paper towel lightly dab the breasts to remove any of the excess moisture. Salt and pepper each breast and sear both sides in a sauté pan. Once you start to get some color on the skin side of the guinea, place it in the oven.

2. Roast about 7 minutes on the first side, turn and roast another 10 minutes, checking to be sure not to overcook. Now remove from the oven and place two pats of butter into the pan.

3. Throw in a bunch of thyme and baste the guinea breasts in pan juices.

4. Serve with fried okra and Sea Island peas for a delicious Middleton Plantation meal.

Guinea Hen, oil on wood by Nancy Ricker Rhett.

MIDDLETON PLACE PORK BELLY & JOHNNY CAKES

SERVES: 4

INGREDIENTS
1 pound cured and smoked pork belly
1 quail egg

JOHNNY CAKES
2 cups Anson Mills Blue cornmeal
2 cups boiling water
1 teaspoon salt

1. Heat pork belly until browned.

2. In a medium bowl, combine the cornmeal, salt and boiling water until it forms a paste.

3. Heat your pan with pork belly drippings. When the pan is hot, spoon the batter into the pan one tablespoon at a time letting it form into cakes, browning on each side until cooked.

4. Once johnny cakes are removed, cut open the quail egg and delicately pour each one into your hot pan cooking through until nicely browned.

5. Place your Johnny cakes, pork belly, and quail egg on the plate and finish with a good quality bourbon infused maple syrup.

FRENCH CHICKEN IN WHITE WINE SAUCE
SERVES: 4

Summer Evenings, oil on canvas by Carol Peek.

Lowcountry cooking is a melting pot of English, West African and French influences with the French influence most prevalent in Charleston. I love this classic French mirepoix to flavor the sauce. The addition of a little prosciutto to the mirepoix gives the sauce an extra depth.

Serve with rice pilaf made with basmati rice, brown or white, known for its perfumed aroma. In the Lowcountry of the Carolinas and Georgia, no dinner is complete without a pilaf. This grain is the bedrock of this region's gumbos, vegetable stews and seafood. Or make it with our prized Carolina Gold Rice.

INGREDIENTS
2 tablespoons butter
4-5 chicken pieces
Kosher salt and freshly ground black pepper
1 tablespoon Hungarian Paprika
1 onion, *finely chopped*
1 carrot, *finely chopped*
1 celery rib, *finely chopped*
2 ounces prosciutto
3/4 cup dry white wine or vermouth
3/4 cup chicken stock
4 tablespoons heavy cream
several sprigs fresh thyme
chopped fresh flat-leaf parsley

1. Melt the butter in a large sauté pan over medium heat. Season the chicken with salt, pepper and paprika then cook 6 - 8 minutes on each side. If cooking chicken breasts, cook them in the skillet with the skin side down to brown them and render the fat from the skin. Remove chicken from the pan.

2. Add the onion, carrot, celery and prosciutto and sauté until the onion is browned and the vegetables are softened. Add wine or vermouth and chicken stock to the pan and stir to combine. Place the chicken back into the pan and bring the liquid to just below a boil. Add sprigs of fresh thyme. Reduce to a simmer and cover with a lid. Simmer the chicken gently in the sauce until cooked through, about 20 minutes, depending on the size of the chicken parts.

3. Remove the chicken from the pan, and boil the liquid to reduce the volume, about 5 minutes. Let the liquid cool slightly and add the cream. Stir to combine and place chicken back into the pan. Cover chicken with sauce and serve over rice or noodles. Sprinkle with parsley.

Previous Page; Broomfield Marsh, oil on canvas by William Means Rhett, Jr..

HOLIDAY CHICKEN SALAD

SERVES: 4-6

Chicken salad just exudes love and Southern hospitality. With these bright red dried cranberries, it just spells holiday time and is sure to bring smiles to faces gathered 'round. 'Tis the time of year we most want to communicate joy through home cooked goodness, and give all who gather a brief respite from the hectic pace of the season. So sit a spell and take time to gather with family and friends and refresh your soul.

1. Combine the chicken, cranberries, celery, onion, apple and slivered almonds. Toss Salad.

2. Combine the remaining ingredients and stir into the chicken mixture. Serve on ciabatta bread or a bed of mixed greens with strawberries and fresh orange slices for garnish.

INGREDIENTS

3 cups cooked chicken, *diced*
1/4 cup dried cranberries
1/2 cup diced celery
3 tablespoons chopped red onion, *finely diced*
1/2 cup Granny Smith apple, *finely diced*
1/4 cup slivered almonds
4-6 tablespoons good mayonnaise
2 tablespoons sour cream
juice of 1/2 lemon
1 teaspoon lemon zest
1/8 teaspoon curry powder
1/4 teaspoon salt
freshly ground black pepper

BRAISED SHORT RIBS ON POLENTA
SERVES: 4

Hankering for some real deep Southern style ribs? You can bet you'll end up with a chin covered in sticky sauce when you bite into these succulent morsels so tender, the meat falls off the bones.

These mouth watering short ribs can be put together in the early morning leaving plenty of time for self indulgence the rest of the day. Boil a few potatoes to mash later in the afternoon with garlic, horseradish and some creamy butter and you have a heart warming combination.

The art of braising is a simple cooking technique with huge outcomes. The main ingredient is seared, or browned in fat, and then simmered in liquid on low heat in a covered pot.

There is no other way to produce deep intense flavors and fork tender texture with the least amount of work. Use this technique for tough cuts of meat such as osso buco, ox-tails and chuck roasts. Serve with sautéed Shitake mushroom on top.

INGREDIENTS

2 1/2 pounds beef short ribs
1 teaspoon Kosher salt
1/2 teaspoon black pepper
1/2 teaspoon ground cinnamon
1/4 tablespoon ground allspice
1 tablespoon olive oil
2 stalks celery, *diced small*
1 medium carrot, *diced small*
1 sweet onion, *diced*
2 tablespoons all-purpose flour
1 cup red wine
1 cup beef broth
1 (14.5 ounce) can diced tomatoes
1 tablespoon tomato paste
3 tablespoons brown sugar
3 tablespoons Worcestershire sauce
2 tablespoons cider vinegar
1/4 teaspoon Tabasco sauce
several bay leaves

1. Preheat the oven to 350°. Score through the connective tissue on the bone-side of the spare ribs until the bone can be seen. Mix together the Kosher salt, black pepper, cinnamon and allspice. Season the meat of the ribs and set aside.

2. Use a large 3 quart stockpot and heat over medium high heat until well heated. Add a little olive oil to the heated pan and tilt to coat. Carefully place ribs into the heated oil and brown completely on all sides. Remove ribs from the pan and set on a plate while browning the vegetables. Add diced vegetables to the pan and season with Kosher salt and freshly ground black pepper. Cook until the vegetables are caramelized and nicely browned. Stir from time to time. Add flour to the vegetables in the pan. This will soak up any oil and form a nice roux.

3. Cook for another few minutes in order to diminish any raw flour taste. Use the red wine to deglaze the pan scraping up any cooked bits. Add diced tomatoes, tomato paste, brown sugar, beef broth, Worcestershire sauce, vinegar, Tabasco sauce and bay leaves.

4. Place in the preheated oven for 2 hours with a tight fitting lid. Cook until meat is tender.

5. If a thicker sauce is desired, remove meat after it has finished cooking and cook the liquid on top of the stove until reduced to the desired thickness.

6. This will vanish in a hurry but if you need to make it ahead of time, it will keep several days in the refrigerator. Serve over mashed potatoes or creamy polenta.

Low Country Splendor, oil on canvas by Michael B. Karas.

PEPPERCORN CRUSTED BEEF TENDERLOIN

SERVES: 4

INGREDIENTS
1 teaspoon whole black peppercorns
1 teaspoon whole green peppercorns
1 teaspoon whole white peppercorns
2 tablespoons butter, *at room temperature*
4 (6 ounce) fillet mignon steaks
(1 1/2 inches thick)
1 teaspoon garlic salt
2 tablespoons olive oil

BLUE CHEESE SAUCE
2 tablespoons olive oil
1/2 pound lump crab-meat, *picked free of cartilage*
1 teaspoon minced garlic
1 shallot, *chopped fine*
3 ounces boursin cheese
1/2 cup half and half
1 tablespoon parmesan cheese
1/4 cup blue cheese, *crumbled*
freshly ground black pepper

1. Place peppercorns in a plastic zip-top bag and crack them on a solid work surface with a mallet until they are broken into small pieces but not pulverized. Scoop them into a bowl, add butter and mix until well combined.

2. Season the steaks all over with garlic salt. Divide the peppercorn butter among the fillets and rub to evenly coat both sides.

3. Heat oil in a large heavy duty skillet over medium high heat until it shimmers, about 2 - 3 minutes. Add the steaks and cook undisturbed to the desired doneness, about 4 minutes per side for medium rare. Transfer steaks to a cutting board and allow to rest at least 5 minutes before serving.

4. BLUE CHEESE SAUCE, Use a heavy duty sauté pan on medium high heat. Add garlic and chopped shallots and cook for about 1 minute. Add crab-meat and cook until heated through.

5. Add the Boursin cheese and melt slowly over low heat. Once melted, add the half and half and gently simmer. Continue to simmer until liquid is reduced to a creamy sauce, about 3 minutes. Add the parmesan cheese and the blue cheese. Season with pepper and serve over the fillets.

PECAN CRUSTED PORK TENDERLOIN

SERVES: 4

INGREDIENTS
3-4 lbs. pork tenderloin
2 tablespoons olive oil
1 cup all purpose flour
1 1/2 cups Panko bread crumbs
¼ cup fresh chopped parsley
1 cup pecans, *chopped fine*
1 teaspoon coarse salt
1/2 teaspoon white pepper
1 teaspoon granulated garlic
2 eggs, *slightly whisked*

CRANBERRY MAPLE SAUCE
1 cup fresh or frozen cranberries
1/2 cup chicken broth
1/2 cup real pure maple syrup
2 teaspoons vinegar
2 teaspoons Dijon mustard
1 teaspoon thyme

1. Rub pork down with olive oil and sear on all sides in hot sauté pan until nicely browned. Allow to cool completely.

2. Place bread crumbs, pecans, salt, pepper and garlic in food processor and pulse a few times to blend well. Add parsley, adjust seasoning if desired.

3. Roll pork in flour first, then egg, making sure pork is well coated. Roll in bread crumbs pressing crumbs onto pork.

4. Preheat oven to 350° until internal temperature reaches 135°, roughly 20-25 minutes. Allow to rest 5 minutes before slicing with sharp knife.

5. CRANBERRY MAPLE SAUCE, Combine the cranberries, chicken broth, maple syrup, cider vinegar, dijon mustard, and thyme into a pan and heat to medium high. Cook, whisking to incorporate the mustard. Continue to cook until the cranberries are softened and the liquid has reduced to a saucy consistency, about 7 minutes. Spoon over slices of tenderloin just before serving.

Oceans Nineteen, oil on canvas by Laurie Meyer.

SERIOUS SOUTHERN STROGANOFF

SERVES: 4

To bump up the mushroom flavor, as well as deepen the color of the stroganoff, I added a half ounce of dried porcini mushrooms, rinsed and minced. With their intense, woodsy flavor, they greatly enrich the broth.

For the braising liquid, I am using chicken broth for its clean and neutral flavor. This dish already has a rich flavor foundation and just needs a little brightening up with the dry white wine or vermouth.

For the creamy sauce which is the hallmark of stroganoff, simply temper the sour cream with a little of the cooking liquid before stirring it back into the pot to finish. Don't be tempted to add the sour cream to the hot mixture without this step or you'll end up with a curdled mess.

1. Add oil to the skillet and heat over medium heat until shimmering but not smoking. Add the minced onions, finely minced carrots, several sprigs of fresh thyme and tomato paste along with 1/4 teaspoon Kosher salt and cook until the vegetables are softened and browned. Stir in the wine, scrapping up any browned bits.

2. Pour the vegetable mixture into the stockpot and add the meat, white mushrooms, broth, soy sauce, tapioca and porcini mushrooms and gently stir to combine. Cover and braise in a 300° oven for 4-6 hours until the meat is fork tender. Length of time will depend on the size of the meat cubes.

3. Scoop up about 1 cup of the liquid in the pot and stir it into sour cream to temper, then pour it back into the stew and stir. Add mustard, season with salt, and freshly ground black pepper to taste. Garnish with freshly chopped parsley and serve on wide buttered noodles or rice.

INGREDIENTS

1 (5 pound) boneless top sirloin tip roast, trimmed and cut into 1 1/2 inch chunks
2 tablespoons canola oil
3 onions, *minced*
2 carrots, *finely minced*
1/4 cup tomato paste
several sprigs of fresh thyme
Kosher salt
3/4 cup dry white wine or vermouth
10 ounces white button mushrooms, *wiped clean, trimmed and sliced*
2 cups chicken broth
1/3 cup soy sauce
1/4 cup Minute tapioca
1/2 ounce dried porcini mushrooms, *rinsed and minced*
1 tablespoon Dijon mustard
1/2 cup sour cream
freshly ground black pepper
2 tablespoons freshly chopped parsley

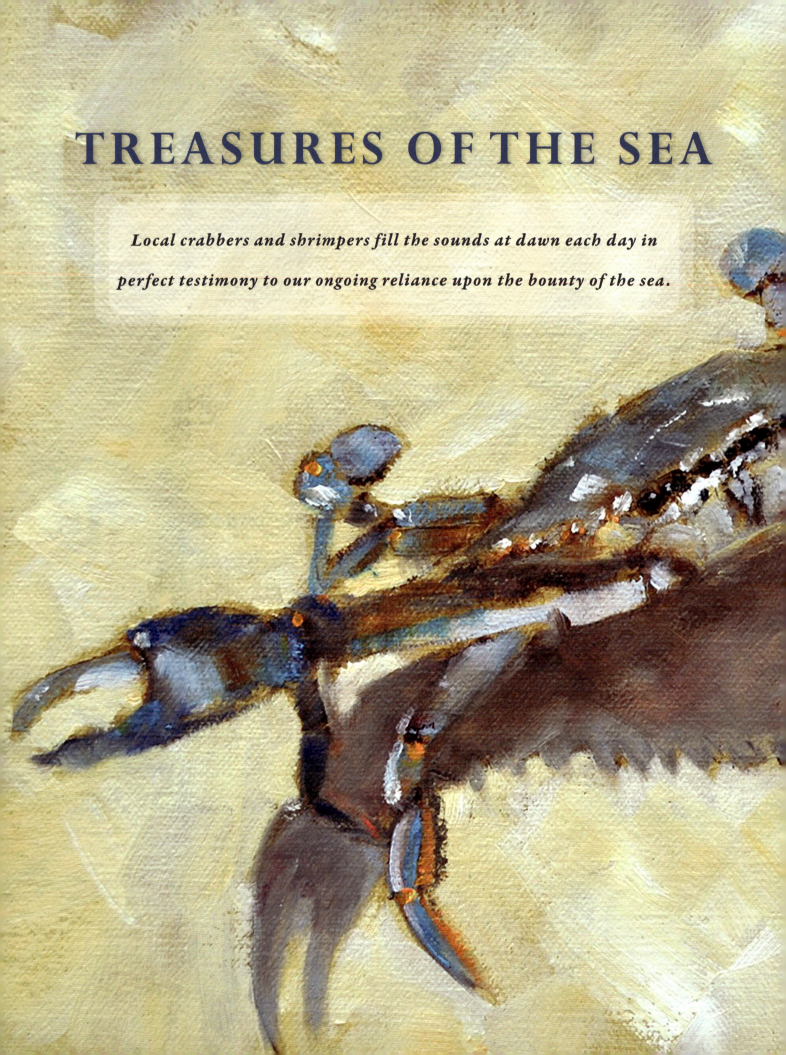

TREASURES OF THE SEA

Local crabbers and shrimpers fill the sounds at dawn each day in perfect testimony to our ongoing reliance upon the bounty of the sea.

Oysters, oil on canvas by Russell Gordon.

Down in the pluff mud of our coastal sounds, the oyster finds a home and sticks with it. Once attached to a hard surface, it will never move. Each spring the male releases his sperm into the water and the female releases her eggs, then it's up to pure chance that somewhere in the sea they will meet and make a new oyster. Once they meet and produce offspring, the larvae are so small that a million can fit in a cupped hand. They will dive in search of something solid to stick to forever, preferably another oyster shell. Then it will stay and grow and never again move. However, if a suitable surface does not exist, the oyster dies. That's reason enough to never deplete our reefs and always recycle the shells.

It wasn't until recently that we realized our sounds cannot survive without the oyster. A single oyster has the ability to filter 50 gallons of water every single day, greatly improving the quality of our water in the process.

Previous Page: Blue Crab, oil on canvas by Shannon Runquist.
Opposite Page: Oyster Bucket, oil on canvas by Michael Harrell.

Mitchelville Beach oil on canvas by Walter Greer.

SEARED AHI TUNA SALAD
SERVES: 2

What makes this dish irresistible is the sparkling clean, fresh from the sea flavor of the tuna which is also meaty, rich and fully satisfying. Serve this ice cold with the crunchy contrast of Napa cabbage drizzled with creamy wasabi dressing for a fabulous meal.

I like to prepare the tuna well in advance of dinner because I love to serve it ice cold. However, it is perfectly fine to prepare and serve it right away.

1. Preheat a skillet large enough to accommodate the tuna steak. Lightly coat the fish with grapeseed oil and season with Kosher salt and freshly ground black pepper. Next coat the fish with sesame seeds pressing them into the fish. Once the oil is hot enough to smoke, add the fish. Cook about 2 minutes per side and promptly remove to a clean plate. Allow it to cool, then wrap and place in the refrigerator until time to serve.

2. CREAMY WASABI DRESSING, Whisk the mayonnaise, wasabi and rice vinegar. Add the sesame oil, water, salt and pepper while continuing to whisk. Now it's time to shred the Napa cabbage. On chilled plates, pile the cabbage to make a nest for the tuna. Using a sharp knife, slice the tuna very thin and place around on the sliced cabbage. Sprinkle with the roasted wasabi peas and drizzle with creamy wasabi dressing. Serve at once.

INGREDIENTS
1 head napa cabbage, *sliced*
1/2 pound fresh Ahi tuna
grapeseed oil
salt and pepper
several tablespoons sesame seeds
1/2 cup roasted wasabi peas

CREAMY WASABI DRESSING
1/2 cup mayonnaise
1/4 cup rice vinegar
2 1/2 tablespoons wasabi powder
1 1/2 teaspoons Asian sesame oil
1 1/2 tablespoons water
Kosher salt and freshly ground black pepper

BLUE CRAB BLISS

Bring a hearty appetite, roll up your sleeves and head out to the Sunbury Crab Company, in Sunbury, Georgia to do some real crab crack-in'. It's been a family owned and operated restaurant for over 20 years.

Sunbury Crab Company is hands down the most unique dining experience in all of South Georgia. It's staunchly no frills with a menu that couldn't be simpler, fried or steamed seafood year round and fire-roasted oysters when the chill hits the salt marshes. Located off the beaten path somewhere in the middle just south of Savannah and north of Jekyll Island. It's a rustic, open-air waterfront seafood dive with one of the most spectacular views anywhere in Coastal Georgia.

The menu is simple and brief. We ordered the steamed blue crab which they served in buckets cleaned and ready to eat. They gave us each a wooden mallet for crackin' and a big piece of parchment paper for a place mat. Sunbury prides itself on pulling their blue crabs right out of the surrounding waters and serving them that same day.

Owner Bernie Maley invited us to climb in the boat and go with him to check the traps. We headed out toward the first crab pot which is a large trap attached to a line and lowered into the water with a white marker attached. That first trap was full of blue crab. He dumped it all into a black plastic bucket on board and grabbed some Menhaden bait fish to refill it, then lowered it back into the blue waters.

Darkness was settling in as the tide ebbed, exposing miles of black pluff mud along either side of the creek. Pungent aromas of the great salt marsh filled the night air. Looking toward the back of the boat I could see a score of great blue herons taking flight, and miles of primitive vistas still untouched by civilization for this is our inheritance. There's a timeless appeal here that reflects the history and character of a community and the generations of fishermen and their families who went before us.

So grab a beer and hang out on the docks as the sun goes down and watch the boats chug along the dockside canal as dusk settles across the land.

No other experience like it. No place. No where.

When we talk about crab, we're talking about blue crab. They are abundant up and down our Eastern Seaboard as far north as Chesapeake Bay and south through Florida and the Gulf Coast. In the South, we look forward to April when they come to us in their most fragile state as soft shells. Don't miss out on the intense goodness of these heavenly creatures. They are one of the sea's greatest gifts to our table.

SHRIMP, CRAB & BEAN SALAD

SERVES: 4

Near Bull Island, oil on canvas by Mark Horton.

Every now and then in the course of salad making a real star is born. I find there is no fortuitous kitchen technique that leads to a stupendous creation, but I do know that a summer spent by the sea invites culinary exploration. The lovely pastel colors of our seafood shades of salmon, apricot, coral and opalescent pearl appeal to the eye as much as the palate. No summer in the Lowcountry is ever complete without casting a shrimp net into our creeks and rivers, wrestling a blue crab off a string into a bucket, braving the high seas or vying for a parking space in front of the local fish market.

The best dishes are quite often nothing more than the artful combinations of a few top quality ingredients beautifully presented so that their essence shines through. Each trip to one of our local farms or farmers markets has been inspirational and I come home eager to convey the purity, simplicity and spirit of that food. I use the ripest tomatoes, the very freshest produce and then treat them with simplicity and respect. A toss with some very good olive oil, a great balsamic with a few shallots or Vidalias, freshly ground black pepper and Fleur de Sel and you're ready.

1. Toss the cooked beans in a bowl with the Vidalia onions, and two tablespoons of the vinaigrette. Sprinkle with some of the basil, salt and pepper. Divide among 4 small serving plates. Ladle the avocado halves with the remaining vinaigrette and season with salt and pepper. Place an avocado half on top of the beans on each plate.

2. Gently stir the crabmeat with 2 tablespoons of the vinaigrette being careful not to break up any lumps. Mound into the avocado halves. Top with the basil chiffonade and lemon zest.

3. Toss shrimp with remaining basil chiffonade and 2 tablespoons vinaigrette and arrange alongside the avocados. Garnish with tomatoes, lemon zest and basil leaves.

INGREDIENTS

12 large wild caught shrimp
1 1/2 cups cooked fresh shell beans
1/2 Vidalia onion, *chopped fine*
1/2 cup Sherry Vinaigrette, *see below*
8 basil leaves, *cut into chiffonade*
Kosher salt and freshly ground black pepper
2 ripe avocados, *halved, pitted and peeled*
1 pound local lump crabmeat
8 cherry tomatoes, *cut in half*
zest of 1/2 lemon
2 ripe avocados, *halved, pitted and peeled*
8 cherry tomatoes, *cut in half*
zest of 1/2 lemon

SHERRY VINAIGRETTE

1/2 shallot finely minced
2 tablespoons sherry vinegar
6 tablespoons extra virgin olive oil
salt and pepper
Whisk together

Mullet Casting, oil on canvas by Michael Harrell.

I love taking beautiful raw ingredients from our waters and cooking them in such a way that it summarizes the sea. Just as important as the endless hours devoted to the perfection of foods is pairing each dish with an incredible painting that evokes a lasting memory. Such devotion and loyalty can only be experienced in an environment as generous as that of the Lowcountry.

MUSSELS MARINIERE
SERVES: 4

For those languorous spells of hot and hotter summer days, we need effortless meals we can prepare quickly. These mussels are fast and simple but make a hearty meal when paired with a loaf of crusty bread to soak up the rich tomato broth.

As a bonus, mussels are a power food packing more iron and Vitamin B12 than beef and are an excellent source of iron.

Just like oysters, they are filter feeders and clean our sounds by filtering over a gallon of water every single hour.

INGREDIENTS

3 tablespoons extra-virgin olive oil
1 1/2 pound mussels
1 tomato, *diced and seeded*
3 cloves garlic
1/2 cup dry white wine or vermouth
1 cup heavy cream
Kosher salt and freshly ground black pepper
1/2 teaspoon red pepper flakes

1. Heat a heavy bottomed sauté pan; add olive oil and mussels.

2. As the mussels open, add the tomato and garlic. Cook the mixture over medium heat for several minutes.

3. Deglaze the pan with white wine or vermouth and reduce the liquid to almost dry. Add cream and reduce to a sauce consistency. Season the mussels with salt and pepper & red pepper flakes.

4. Discard any mussels that are unopened after 8 minutes of cooking. Serve immediately with crusty bread.

SOFT SHELL CRAB

SERVES: 4

Inspired by Chef Robert Wysong of Colleton River Plantation

INGREDIENTS
4 soft shell blue crabs
all-purpose flour
Kosher salt and freshly ground black pepper
peanut oil

SEAFOOD SPICE
1 tablespoon Old Bay seasoning
2 teaspoon sugar
1 teaspoon ground coriander
1 teaspoon salt
1 teaspoon freshly ground black pepper
Blend all together

REMOULADE SAUCE
1 cup good mayonnaise
1 tablespoon fresh lemon juice
1 tablespoon sweet pickle relish
1/2 tablespoon capers, *finely minced*
1/2 tablespoon flat leaf parsley, *washed & minced*
1/2 tablespoon Worcestershire
1/2 teaspoon smoked paprika
1/2 teaspoon Tabasco

1. Prepare crabs and dust with seasoned flour. Carefully fry in heated oil, 325° until golden brown.

2. Remove and drain on a paper towel.

3. Season liberally with seafood spice mixture. Split in half and arrange with lemon slices and whole leaf parsley for garnish. Serve with remoulade on the side.

JAMBALAYA STRUDEL

SERVES: 8-10

Inspired by Chef Tom Ferrell of Berkeley Hall.

INGREDIENTS
3 tablespoons butter
1/2 medium green pepper, *diced*
1/2 medium red pepper, *diced*
1/2 medium onion, *small diced*
2 thick strips pork bacon, *minced*
6 ounces smoked Andoullie sausage links, *minced*
1 1/2 cup brown rice
2 tablespoons tomato paste
1/4 teaspoon cayenne pepper
1/2 tablespoon paprika
4 1/2 cups chicken stock
1 small bay leaf
1/2 teaspoon dry thyme
1 small cooked chicken breast
1 teaspoon chopped garlic
3/4 pound raw local baby shrimp, *peeled and chopped fine*
1 tomato, *core removed and diced*
2 tablespoons fresh chopped parsley
1 package Pepperidge Farm Puff Pastry sheets
1/4 cup flour
1 egg, *slightly whisked*

MUSTARD WINE SAUCE
2 shallots minced
1/2 cup white wine, chardonnay
3 cups heavy cream
1/2 teaspoon cayenne pepper
Pinch of coarse salt
1/3 cup Grey Poupon mustard
Whisk until thoroughly combined

1. Place butter in 2 quart heavy bottomed sauce pan. Melt butter and sauté peppers and onions with bacon for 5 minutes, stirring occasionally. Add Andoullie sausage, brown rice, tomato paste, cayenne pepper, and paprika; stir to blend ingredients. Add chicken stock, bay leaf and thyme. Stir once, cover and simmer until broth is almost gone. Add chicken, garlic, shrimp, tomato and parsley. Stir again. Cover and simmer 3-4 minutes or until rice absorbs all broth. Lay out on sheet tray and allow to cool.

2. On counter sprinkle small amount of flour and on puff pastry sheets. Roll out slightly forming a rectangle. Place pile of cooled rice mixture in center of pastry, leaving about 4 inches of dough not covered around rice. Brush egg around edges of dough.

3. Gently fold bottom of pastry up over rice mixture, then top of pastry down. Fold both sides in over rice, so now rice is completely sealed. Gently roll over onto buttered sheet tray. Using puff pastry box as guide, shape strudel to about the same diameter.

4. Brush top of strudel with remaining egg and bake in a 350° oven until golden brown. Allow to cool 5 minutes before slicing on the diagonal. Top with mustard wine sauce and serve on fresh spinach leaves.

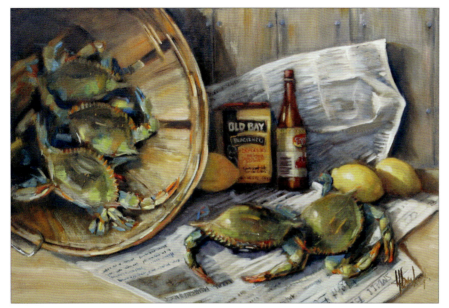

Dinner Plans, oil on canvas by Hilarie Lambert.

CRAZY CRAB BENEDICT

SERVES: 8-10

"If it ain't Southern, it ain't coming in the door," says Chef Sean Brock of Charleston's Husk.

Husk has been hailed as possibly the most important restaurant in the history of Southern cooking. Time will tell but the culture of the restaurant was clear from the start. Mr. Brock is a son of the South and believes the finest cooking must contain locally grown and harvested products from either land or sea.

By definition, Mr. Brock is a locavore – a person who wants to eat only food that is grown within a radius of 100 miles from their dinner table. Local foods are becoming increasingly popular because they are fresher, healthier and more beneficial to the environment and the local economy. Local fruits and vegetables are less likely to be waxed, dyed or ripened with ethylene gas and they are by far more flavorful. Picked at the height of freshness, often making it to market within 24 hours of being picked, while food from non-local sources may have been in transit for more than 7 days and warehoused for many months.

Here is an amazing recipe that can be made simply and quickly with nothing but fresh, local ingredients. It's quaranteed to be a huge hit and the Hollandaise is the perfect sauce for crab – buttery, lemony perfection. This classic brunch dish also makes a great supper when paired with a simple green salad.

INGREDIENTS

1/4 cup finely chopped spring onions
1/8 cup finely chopped bell pepper
1/2 cup good mayonnaise
1 teaspoon Worcestershire sauce
3/4 teaspoon Tabasco sauce
Juice of 1/2 lemon
2 tablespoons freshly chopped parsley
salt and freshly ground black pepper to taste
2 cup very fresh lump crabmeat, *picked free of cartilege and shells*

HOLLANDAISE SAUCE

2 egg yolks
4 tablespoons cream
4 large tablespoons butter, *softened*
Juice of 1/2 lemon
1 tablespoon white vinegar
1/8 teaspoon sugar
dash of salt and cayenne

POACHED EGGS

4 cups water
1 tablespoon white vinegar
4 eggs

1. Whisk together all ingredients except the crab and red peppers. Gently fold in the crab and peppers being careful not to break up the crab too much. Reserve.

2. HOLLANDAISE SAUCE, Combine all ingredients, except the vinegar, in the top of a double boiler, over boiling water. Whisk until thick, about 3 minutes and set aside. Do not reheat or cover the pot. Thin the mixture with a small amount of chicken broth if needed. Stir in the vinegar.

3. Bring the water, vinegar and salt to a low simmer in a medium saucepan. Crack an egg into a small dish and gently slide the egg into the water. Crack another egg into the same dish and while the water returns to a low simmer, slide the second egg into the water. Repeat and let simmer until the eggs are set. Count on about 2 to 3 minutes. Remove with a slotted spoon onto a paper towel lined plate

4. Top a slice of whole grain toast or a fresh biscuit with a poached egg. Add a small scoop of the crab salad on top of the egg. Top with hollandaise sauce.

"I love the marsh," author Pat Conroy says nodding towards a sweep of spartina grass. *"I don't know of any place that smells like this. It's a magnificent smell. It's the smell of where all life comes from. I love that all shrimp, all crab, all oysters are born in the marsh."*

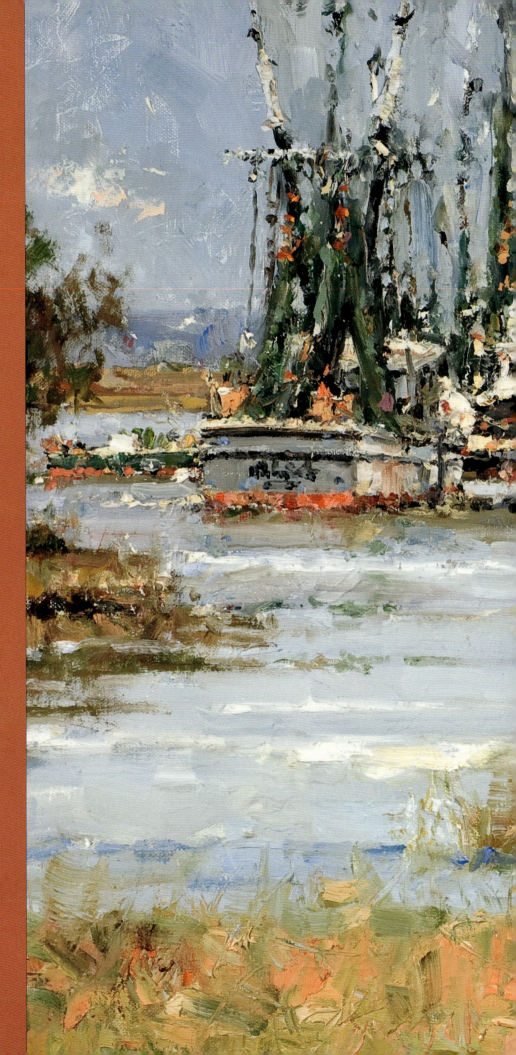

Shrimpers St. Helena,
oil on canvas by Peter Rolfe.

BLACKENED MAHI ON TOMATO COULIS

SERVES: 4

Inspired by Hudson's Seafood House on the Docks.

INGREDIENTS
4 Mahi fillets, 7 ounces each
blackening seasoning, *see below*
2 ounces fresh jumbo crab-meat
1 cup cooked fresh spinach
2 tablespoons mayonnaise
2 tablespoons parmesan cheese

Blackened Seasoning
1 heaping tablespoon Hungarian paprika
2 teaspoons Kosher salt
1 heaping teaspoon garlic powder
1 heaping teaspoon onion powder
1/4 - 1/2 teaspoon cayenne pepper
2 teaspoons black pepper
1/2 teaspoon fresh thyme
12 teaspoon fresh oregano
Whisk Together

1. Preheat oven to 350°. Lightly season with blackening seasoning. Sauté fillets in pan on both sides for about one minute.

2. In a mixing bowl, add mayonnaise, crab, cooked spinach and Parmesan. Remove fish from pan and place spinach mixture on top. Cook in oven for about 8 minutes.

3. Tomato Coulis - Toss 3 vine ripe tomatoes in extra virgin olive oil, salt and pepper. Then roast tomatoes at 350° for 20 minutes. Roast garlic cloves in extra virgin olive oil for about 15 minutes. Let cool and put into blender with tomatoes. Add 1/4 cup chicken stock and 1/4 cup cream. Blend until smooth. Place on the plate, and add the fish and top with crab mixture.

AMEN STREET SHRIMP & GRITS

SERVES: 2-4

Inspired by Chef Ramon Taimanglo of Amen Street Fish & Raw Bar

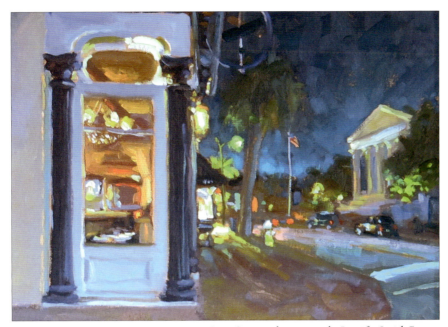

Amen Street, oil on canvas by Jennifer Smith Rogers.

INGREDIENTS

1/2 cup Tasso Ham, *ground in a food processor*
2 tablespoons green onions, *sliced thin*
3/4 cup heavy cream
1 batch roasted tomato puree
12 large shrimp
1 cup Stone-Ground Grits

ROASTED TOMATO PUREE

3 vine ripened tomatoes, *cut into wedges*
1 tablespoon garlic, *minced*
2 tablespoon shallot, *sliced thin*
4 tablespoons red wine vinegar
3 tablespoons molasses
2 tablespoons olive oil

GRITS

4 cups water
1/2 cup cream
3 tablespoons butter
salt and pepper to taste
1 cup stone ground grits

From seafood shacks to old neighborhood pubs, the South Carolina and Georgia coast is a foodie mecca.

If you're in the heart of downtown Charleston and you hear an "amen" as you pass by the corner of East Bay and Cumberland, it's likely to be a happy diner praising the blessings of the sea at Amen Street Fish and Raw Bar at 205 E. Bay Street.

Local lore says Amen Street was so named because amens could be heard coming from neighboring churches. You'll say amen and hallelujah once you step inside and taste Chef Ramon's celebrated Shrimp and Grits.

1 TOMATO PUREE, Place tomatoes on a baking rack and season with salt and pepper. Roast in a 500° oven for 20 minutes. Let rest to room temperature and remove skin and seeds. Rough chop. In a sauce pan, place the garlic and shallots with 2 tablespoons olive oil and sauté for 2 minutes. Add tomatoes, red wine vinegar and molasses and turn heat to medium. Cook stirring constantly until most of the liquid has evaporated and set aside.

2 GRITS, Bring water and butter to a boil, slowly whisking in grits. Turn heat to low and cook 20 minutes, stirring to prevent sticking. Whisk in cream and rest 10 minutes before serving.

3 Place a large sauté skillet on burner over medium high heat. Once pan is warm add 2 tablespoons oil. Then add shrimp. Sauté 1 minutes on each side. Add tasso and tomato puree, then pour over grits to serve.

SPOONFULS OF COMFORT

Summer Day, oil on canvas by Rhett Thurman.

VIC'S FRENCH ONION SOUP

SERVES: 4

Vic's, a fine dining restaurant, has become a favorite of mine whenever visiting Savannah, a city of old world southern charm. It's housed in an 18th century cotton warehouse at Factor's Walk on Bay Street overlooking the river. The original pulleys used to lower cotton from the warehouse to the ships on the river below can still be seen from the outside of the building.

INGREDIENTS

5 sprigs fresh thyme
5 sprigs parsley
2 bay leaves
1/2 stick butter
5 Vidalia onions or other sweet onions, *julienned*
3 cloves garlic, *minced*
1 1/2 teaspoons salt
1/2 cup all-purpose flour
1/2 cup dry red wine
1/2 cup dry sherry
1/2 cup bourbon
4 cups Veal stock or chicken stock
salt and pepper to taste
4 (1 inch slices French bread)
granulated garlic to taste
4 slices Gruyere cheese

1. Make a bouquet garni by tying the thyme springs, parsley sprigs and bay leaves together. Melt 1/2 cup butter in a heavy saucepan over medium-low heat. Add the onions, garlic cloves and 1 1/2 teaspoons salt and cook for 1 hour or until caramelized. Whisk in the flour to make a roux and cook for 3 minutes or until light brown, stirring constantly. Whisk in the wine, sherry, bourbon and the stock. Add the bouquet garni and bring to a boil, stirring constantly. Reduce the heat and simmer for 1 hour. Season with salt and pepper.

2. Preheat the oven to 400°. Arrange the French bread slices on a baking sheet. Brush each slice with some of the 2 tablespoons melted butter and sprinkle with salt, pepper and granulated garlic. Bake until golden brown.

3. Remove the bouquet garni and ladle the soup into oven-proof bowls, filling about 3/4 full. Top each serving with a slice of toasted bread and add a slice of cheese. Broil until the cheese is brown and bubbly. Let stand for 5 minutes before serving.

Basic Chicken Stock

"Indeed, stock is everything in cooking, at least in French cooking. Without it, nothing can be done. If one's stock is good, what remains of the work is easy; if on the other hand, it is bad or mediocre, it is quite hopeless to expect anything approaching a satisfactory result."

- Auguste Escoffier

If you want to raise your level of cooking expertise from pedestrian to gourmand, learn to make the flavorful foundation to all your soups, stews, and gravies. Master the technique of making stock.

INGREDIENTS

1 large stockpot, 16 quart
2 roasting chickens
3 large yellow onions, *peeled and quartered*
6 carrots, *peeled*
5 stalks celery, *chopped*
6 parsnips, *cut in half*
1 bunch parsley (about 20 sprigs)
12 sprigs fresh thyme
1 head garlic, *unpeeled and cut in half crosswise*
2 tablespoons Kosher salt
3 teaspoons whole black peppercorns
4 bay leaves
5 quarts water

Place chickens and the rest of the ingredients into a 16 quart stockpot. Add 5 quarts of water and bring to a boil. Simmer uncovered for 4 hours. Strain the entire contents of the pot through a colander and discard the solids. Chill the stock overnight. The next day remove the surface fat. Use immediately or pack in containers and freeze for up to 3 months.

SEA ISLAND SHRIMP BISQUE
SERVES: 4

Nothing says comfort food like a piping hot bowl of soup. Try this on a frigid winter day with a grilled cheese sandwich for dipping. Bite sized chunks of shrimp add texture and interest to this sumptuous Lowcountry specialty. Michael Karas' work, as seen below, best captures the majestic nature of such a winter morning sunrise with his use of subtle yellow throughout the sky.

1. Bring 3 cups water to a boil and add the shrimp. Cover and bring to a second boil. Ladle shrimp out of the water and rinse under cold water. Shell and devein the shrimp and cut them into small pieces. Using a food processor fitted with a steel blade, finely mince half the shrimp. Cover and refrigerate until needed. Return the shells to the cooking liquid. Bring it back to a boil and cook until it is reduced to 2 cups. Strain the broth and discard the shells.

2. Use a paper towel to wipe out the pot and add the butter and the finely minced onion. Sauté until softened, about 5 minutes. Stir in the flour and cook, stirring, until smooth. Slowly stir in the broth, milk and half and half. Season well with salt and a dash of cayenne pepper. Bring to a simmer, stirring constantly, and reduce the heat to low. Simmer, stirring often for about 20 - 25 minutes.

3. Add the remaining shrimp and cook until they are just heated, about 2 minutes. Adjust seasonings to taste. Serve adding a tablespoon of sherry to each serving. Garnish each serving with a slice of lemon, if desired.

INGREDIENTS

4 cups shellfish broth
1 pound fresh local shrimp
3 tablespoons butter
1 onion, *finely minced*
1 heaping tablespoon all-purpose flour
2 cups whole milk
1 cup half and half
dash cayenne pepper
Kosher salt and freshly ground black pepper
6 tablespoons dry sherry

Resplendent Morning, oil on canvas by Michael B. Karas.

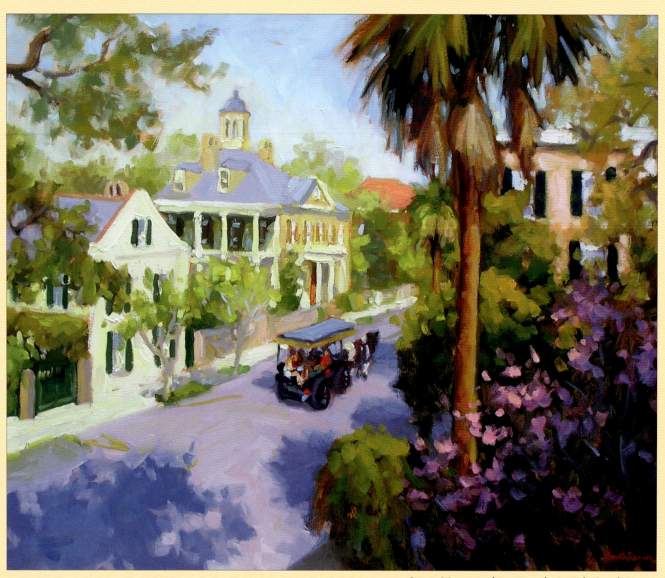

Lower Meeting, oil on canvas by Jennifer Smith Rogers.

You can shake the sand from your shoes,

but it will never leave your soul.

SHE CRAB SOUP

SERVES: 12-14

Inspired by Chef Kevin Cavanaugh of the South Carolina Yacht Club.

> *"Use only the best fresh regional ingredients and keep it simple."*
> *- James Beard*

The illustrious James Beard was not referring specifically to soup when he administered this culinary advice, but his wisdom is certainly pertinent. Soup is the ultimate comfort food and our farmers' markets are the best places to find the freshest vegetables and fruits of the season. They offer all the inspiration I need to cook something special for dinner. Cold blustery winter nights lose their chill when we curl up by the fire with a bowl of delicious bisque or chowder. I believe that soup making is the most gratifying culinary experience. Gentle stirring and simmering can't help but bring forth the nurturing instincts of every soup maker, and the finished product has the power to sooth the soul in truly magical ways.

Our delight in food reaches far beyond the plate. The simple act of slicing, chopping, tasting, and adding seasonings that make it all come together becomes an act of contentment rather than a chore to be dreaded and hurried along.

1. Make a sachet of cheesecloth containing parsley, bay leaves, fennel seed and tarragon.

2. In a large stock pot melt butter; then add carrots, fennel, onions, bell pepper, celery, leeks and garlic. Sweat until onions are soft and clear, being careful not to brown. Incorporate flour, whisking to create a roux.

3. Add sachet, sherry, clam juice, and lobster stock. Bring to a boil and reduce liquids by 1/4. Add tomato paste, cream, and half and half. Bring to almost a boil. Reduce to a simmer. Add roe and simmer for 25 minutes. Remove sachet and blend. Season to taste.

4. Garnish with jumbo lump crab-meat, red bell pepper, fennel and corn kernels.

INGREDIENTS

1/4 pound unsalted butter
1 1/2 cup flour
2 carrots, *diced*
1 fennel bulb, *diced*
2 yellow onions, *diced*
1 red bell pepper, *diced*
3 stalks celery, *diced*
1 leek, *julienned*
1 tablespoon garlic
1/2 bunch parsley
2 bay leaves
2 tablespoons fennel seeds
1/2 cup fresh tarragon
2 cups cooking sherry
2 quarts clam juice
2 cups lobster stock
2 tablespoons tomato paste
3/4 cup blue crab meat
2 cups heavy cream
2 cups half and half
2 ounces crab roe

CAROLINA BRUNSWICK STEW

SERVES: 10

Growing up, every time we gathered with our North Carolina family down by the river, we'd have Brunswick Stew with Hush-puppies and Buttermilk Cornbread. My father and Uncle Herman would smoke the pork and chicken all afternoon to make it just right for this delicious stew. The smoked taste of the chicken and pork, and especially this stew, is the flavor of my childhood.

Now it has become a staple, served piping hot, at every backyard oyster roast.

1. Melt butter, then add the diced onions and garlic and sweat until translucent, about 15 minutes. Stir in the ketchup, yellow mustard, white vinegar, and brown sugar, Worcestershire, Tabasco and salt and pepper and simmer in a 2 quart saucepan over low heat. Simmer the sauce about 10 minutes. Then turn off the heat, and set aside to be added later.

2. Use a large stockpot and sauté the ground round over medium heat. Once nicely browned add the home made sauce until well combined and simmer.

3. Add the diced smoked pork and/or shredded chicken. Next add the sweet mustard based barbecue sauce. You will want to cover the meats completely with the sauces. Cook for another 10 to 15 minutes on low heat. Add the tomatoes, corn, Yukon Gold potatoes and beans and let simmer for a few hours on medium heat, adding the chicken stock to thin as needed. Stew can be made as thick as you like it or thinned out. Add the Texas Pete to taste.

4. Serve with warm southern buttermilk cornbread for a special winter's night supper.

INGREDIENTS

1 teaspoon cayenne pepper
freshly ground black pepper
sea salt
1 cup sweet mustard-based barbecue sauce
2 pounds ground round, diced smoked pork, or a combination
1 pound poached or smoked chicken shredded
2 large cans diced tomatoes
1 pound sweet corn
1 pound butter bean
4 cups diced Yukon Gold potatoes
4 cups homemade chicken stock
Texas Pete Hot Sauce - to taste

SAUCE

1/4 cup butter
1 3/4 ketchup
1/4 cup French's Yellow Mustard
1/4 cup white vinegar
1/4 cup Worcestershire sauce
1/4 cup dark brown sugar
2 cloves garlic, *crushed*
dash of Tabasco to taste
Kosher salt
freshly ground black pepper
3 cups sweet onions, *finely diced*

Opposite Page: Bucket Load,
Oil on Canvas by Michael Harrell.

Flight, oil on canvas by Mark Horton.

ST. SIMONS CRAB STEW

SERVES: 6-8

Avenue of Oaks, oil on canvas by Mildred Nix Huie.

You'll have Georgia on your mind after a visit to this coastal retreat. It's home to Mildred Huie Wilcox, one of St. Simon's most venerated citizens: Community Arts Advocate, Humanitarian and International Art Scholar. This is the Crab Stew served at plantations throughout the 18th century, researched and updated by Ms. Wilcox.

1. Melt butter in a large stockpot over medium heat. Add celery and cook until softened. Stir in flour to make a smooth roux. Cook for 3 minutes.

2. Gradually whisk in the heavy cream, stir in broth, bring to a simmer and pour in the white wine.

3. Season with dill, old bay seasoning, Worcestershire and hot sauce. Simmer, covered for 10 minutes. Add crab-meat, lemon juice and simmer for another few minutes. Ladle into bowls and top off with chopped hard boiled eggs and parsley.

INGREDIENTS

- 1/2 cup plus 2 tablespoons butter
- 10 tablespoons all-purpose flour
- 2 stalks celery, *finely minced*
- Kosher salt and freshly ground black pepper
- 1 quart heavy cream
- 1 1/2 cups chicken broth
- 2 teaspoons hot pepper sauce
- 4 teaspoons Worcestershire sauce
- 2 tablespoons fresh dill, *chopped*
- 1 teaspoon Old Bay Seasoning
- 1 pound lump crab-meat
- 1/2 fresh lemon, *squeezed*
- 1/4 cup chopped fresh parsley
- 1/2 cup white wine
- 6 hard boiled eggs, *peeled and chopped for garnish*

Picnic Basket, oil on canvas by C.W. Mundy.

Still life with Squash, oil on canvas by John Encinias.

BISQUE OF WINTER SQUASH
SERVES: 8-10

The kitchen will quickly fill with the tantalizing aroma of leeks, and squash roasting in the oven. What makes this soup so flavorful is that the veggies are roasted in advance. This process concentrates and caramelize flavors. Then the ingredients are puréed in a blender until smooth. Just before serving, top it off with some creamy Mascarpone cream.

INGREDIENTS
1 pound butternut squash, *peeled, seeded and diced*
1 sweet potato, *peeled and diced*
1 medium onion
2 leeks, *trimmed cleaned and diced*
2 tablespoons olive oil
2 carrots
4-6 cups chicken broth
1 cup half and half
1 tablespoon fresh thyme, *chopped*
Mascarpone cream for topping

1 Preheat oven to 425°. Peel and dice the squash, sweet potato, onion, and the leeks uniformly, about 1/2 inches. Toss with olive oil and spread pieces onto a large flat foil lined baking pan. Season with salt and pepper and thyme. Roast for about 40 minutes until all veggies are tender.

2 Place roasted mixture into a blender with about half the broth and puree. Add more broth to desired degree of thickness, and the half and half. Purée. Transfer to a saucepan and reheat gently. Serve with a swirl of mascarpone cream for a perfect garnish.

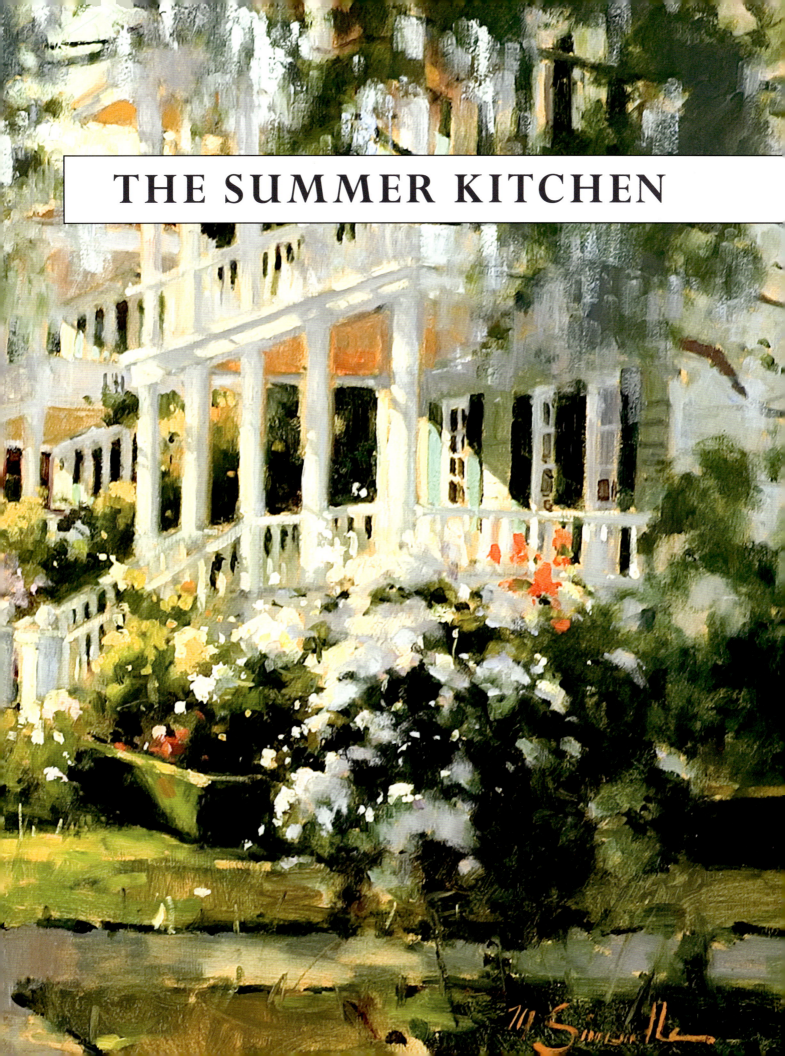

THE SUMMER KITCHEN

SWEET CORN CHOW-CHOW
YIELDS: 5 JARS

Inspired by Chef Trey Dutton of Palmetto Bluff.

What a joy to take beautiful raw ingredients from our beloved sea islands, and seal them in jars of strawberry-rhubarb jam, sweet corn chow-chow and fresh pickles as memories of summer.

"Putting Up" according to Trey Dutton, is a true Southern tradition and plays a major role in Southern hospitality.

With roots deep in the heart of south Georgia's farm country, Trey Dutton, Chef de Cuisine of Palmetto Bluff developed a passion for anything and everything that can be canned. On a recent visit he showed me everything from pickled kumquats and key limes to strawberry-rhubarb jam and his grandmother's pickle relish.

During our time together he shared his fondest memories of visiting his grandparents in a place where front porches were wide, words were long, tall glasses of iced tea were served often and someone's heart was always being blessed. Best of all there was always a large stockpot simmering on the stove where the family gathered around sharing ideas for canning and creating jars of deliciousness to be shared with friends and neighbors. That was Southern hospitality at its finest and what was talked about out on the front porch after supper.

INGREDIENTS

8 cups sweet summer corn, *cut off the cob*
4 cups sweet Vidalia onions, *diced small*
4 cups red bell pepper, *diced small*
4 cups green tomatoes, *diced small*
1 cup roasted red pepper, *minced*
2 cups sugar
1/2 cup blackening spice
4 cups cider vinegar
fresh cilantro

1. Combine all ingredients in a medium sauce pot and simmer over medium heat until almost dry. Stir frequently.

2. When desired consistency is reached, pour into sterilized jars, seal, and process in boiling water for 10 minutes.

3. Fold in fresh chopped cilantro when ready to use. Use 1 tablespoon per cup of Chow-Chow.

Previous Page: Beaufort Beauties, oil on canvas by Marilyn Simandle.

PLANTATION PICKLED OKRA
SERVES: 5

It's summertime – time to think fresh okra, fried chicken, red rice, deviled eggs, potato salad, boiled ocean-fresh shirmp, and decadent sweets. Okra is a special Lowcountry treat. Indeed, gathering dusty green pods from the vines while surrounded by windswept ocean vistas is one of the great pleasures of living by the shore.

I have never been quite certain whether there is something unusual and mysterious in our soil or perhaps our salt-misted air, but vegetables along our coast are the best tasting, intensely flavored in the entire world. Certainly living here with the abundance of spectacular vegetables is one of the very nicest things about life in the Lowcountry.

INGREDIENTS
1 pound okra, *trimmed and slice in half lengthwise*
6 tablespoons Kosher salt
3 cups distilled white vinegar
2 tablespoons sugar
2 bay leaves
1 tablespoon pickling spice
1/4 teaspoon cayenne pepper
2 medium onions, *halved lengthwise, cut into 1/2 inch thick slices*
1 fresh jalapeño, *stemmed and seeded*

1 Rinse okra in a colander and toss with 3 tablespoons Kosher salt. Let the okra drain in the colander for 10 to 15 minutes. Prepare an ice-water bath and set aside. Use a non-reactive pan – stainless steel or enamel work well. Place the rest of the salt, 2 cups water, vinegar, sugar, bay leaves, pickling spice, cayenne, onions, and jalapeños into a medium saucepan. Bring to a boil over medium heat, stirring until the sugar has dissolved.

2 Rinse okra under cold water to remove salt and transfer to a large bowl. Pour brine over okra and set bowl in the ice water bath. Let it cool 10 minutes. Transfer bowl to refrigerator to cool completely for about 30 minutes.

> *Oyster season has ended, the marsh grass begins to turn from shades of golden brown to green, for summer has arrived in the Lowcountry.*

Ashepoo Marshland, oil on canvas by Betty Anglin Smith.

Set up for Breakfast, oil on canvas by Hilarie Lambert.

SWEET POTATO BUTTER

YIELDS: 6 JARS

INGREDIENTS

6 cups sweet potatoes, *diced and peeled*

2 cups Granny Smith apples, *diced and peeled*

4 cups water

2/3 cups orange juice concentrate

zest of 1 orange

1/2 cup packed dark brown sugar

1 1/2 teaspoons ground cinnamon

1 teaspoon ground nutmeg

1/2 teaspoon ground cloves

1 In a heavy saucepan, combine all ingredients and mix well. Bring to a boil and reduce heat. Simmer uncovered for 2 to 2 1/4 hours or until mixture is thickened and about 1 cup of liquid remains. Stir frequently.

2 Using an immersion blender, blend everything until smooth. Transfer to jars or containers and store in refrigerator for up to a month.

PEACH GINGER JAM

YIELDS: 8-10 JARS

Peaches in Gullah Basket, watercolor on paper by Nancy Ricker Rhett.

INGREDIENTS

3 pounds peaches
3 cups sugar
3 tablespoons chopped fresh ginger
2 teaspoons lemon juice
1/4 teaspoon allspice
1 teaspoon pure vanilla extract

1. Take out a non-reactive pot either ceramic or stainless steel. Place the peaches in boiling water for 1 minute or until the skins loosen.

2. Plunge them in ice water. Slip off the skins and halve the fruit and remove pits.

3. Cut the peaches into small 1 inch pieces. Combine peaches with the sugar, ginger, lemon juice and allspice.

4. Simmer over medium heat for 30 minutes or until the mixture is thick enough to mound on the back of a spoon. Ladle into jars and store in the fridge for up to 2 months.

THE SUMMER KITCHEN

Watermelon, oil on canvas by Loran Speck.

CHICKEN & WATERMELON SALAD

SERVES: 5

Watermelon is the ultimate Southern summer treat. It's synonymous with summer picnics and barbecues with everyone grabbing slices of this luscious fruit and chowing down all the way to the green rind.

While watermelon may not have originated in the South, Southerners can proudly say it was perfected here. Southern food historian John Egerton believes African slaves brought the watermelon to the colonies along with other Southern staples such as okra, collard greens, peanuts and black-eyed peas. West Africa has had the single largest influence on Lowcountry cooking.

1 Sauté chicken in grape seed oil. In a shallow bowl, combine chicken and buttermilk. In a separate bowl combine the flour cracker meal, and salt and pepper. Dredge the chicken coated in buttermilk in the mixture and fry until cooked through.

2 LIME VINAIGRETTE DRESSING, In a jar with a lid, shake together the ingredients. Add the fresh mint and basil just before serving along with the dressing. Toss gently.

INGREDIENTS

4 boneless chicken breasts, *cut into strips*
1 cup buttermilk
1/4 cup all-purpose flour
1 cup cracker meal
pinch of sea salt
freshly ground black pepper
grape seed oil

Salad

4 cups watermelon, *cubed*
1/4 feta cheese, *crumbled*
1/4 red onion, *sliced*
1 cup strawberries, *cut into quarters*

Lime vinaigrette dressing

4 tablespoons olive oil
4 tablespoons fresh lime juice
1 teaspoon Dijon mustard
1/4 teaspoon ground cumin
1/4 teaspoon salt
freshly ground black pepper
a handful of fresh chopped mint and basil

RUSTIC HEIRLOOM TOMATO SALAD
SERVES: 5

A perfect vine-ripe tomato, bursting with the earthy sweetness of summertime, is held in holy reverence by Southerners.

Summer in the South is a time for picnicking and grilling. Let's have casual meals that are fuss free and feature the season's freshest flavors such as delicious Silver Queen corn, tomatoes, cucumbers, zucchini and our wonderful field peas. They are, after all, the components of dishes of great pride for us Southerners and there's bound to be a gracious plenty of them at all our gatherings.

This is the old fashioned salad I grew up with made only in July and August when the ingredients are perfect. Avoid tomatoes that have been refrigerated. This greatly diminishes their flavor.

INGREDIENTS
2 pounds heirloom tomatoes
1/2 red onion

DRESSING
3 tablespoons white balsamic vinegar
2 tablespoons extra virgin olive oil
1 tablespoon honey
2 tablespoons fresh mint, *chopped*
3 tablespoons fresh basil, *chopped*
1/2 Sea salt
1/4 teaspoon freshly ground black pepper
1/4 cup feta cheese & croûtons optional

1. Coarsely chop up the tomatoes being sure to remove any stems or rough patches. Thinly slice the onion and wash the leaves of the herbs picked from their stems. Toss herbs, tomatoes and onion together in a large bowl.

2. DRESSING, Whisk together the ingredients for the dressing. Pour over the top of the tomatoes and serve immediately. You will not want to make this ahead of time and stick it in the fridge because the tomatoes will get mealy and lose their wonderful smooth texture. Yields: 4-6 servings.

3. Make your own croûtons with what baker's often call "country bread." Cut off the crusty outside and tear the insides into nice big pieces. Then place all the pieces on a cookie sheet, toss with some olive oil, some sea salt and pepper and pop them into a 400° oven. Once they get all toasty and golden, take them out. Add the croûtons to the bowl of tomatoes at the very last minute before tossing.

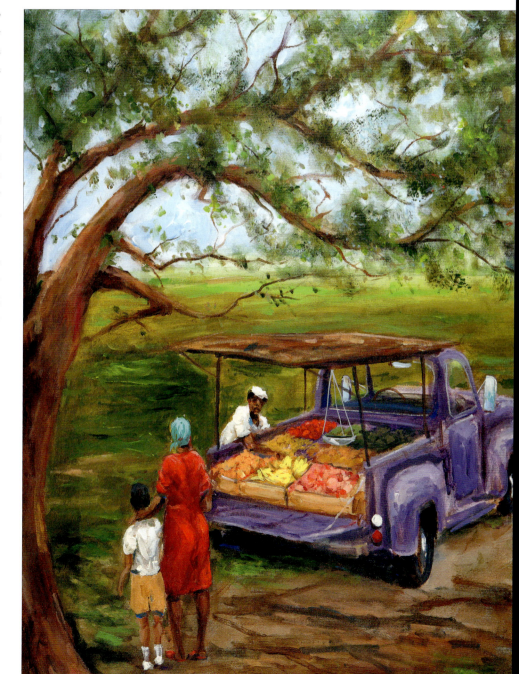

Produce from Cart,
oil on canvas by Ted Ellis.

STRAWBERRY - RHUBARB JAM
YIELDS: 5 JARS

Here's a simple way to prepare the jars for canning. You may first sanitize them in your dishwasher or sink. Next heat your oven to 225° to 250° and place the jars and lids in a pan and allow them to stay in the oven for at least 10 minutes or until ready to fill.

Waking up in the summertime to the smell of homemade biscuits and sizzling bacon is the best kind of alarm clock. And if those biscuits are slathered with a generous amount of homemade strawberry-rhubarb jam, its even better. After a full Southern breakfast, a kayak trip down the waterway through the marshlands is my idea of a perfect summer day.

My desire to stretch the deliciousness of summer into the fall and winter months ahead is always on my mind. One way to stretch the season is with this jam of beautiful sun-ripened berries. Don't limit this jam to the usual morning toast or croissant, it is also a delicious finishing glaze for roasted chicken or sweetener for homemade vinaigrettes.

INGREDIENTS
1 quart ripe strawberries
1 1/2 pounds fully ripe rhubarb
1/2 cup water
1 box fruit pectin
1/2 teaspoon butter
1 vanilla bean, *scraped*
juice of 1 lemon
6 cups sugar, *measured into a separate bowl*

1 Prepare strawberries by removing stems and cutting them in half. Crush them until crushed but chunky by using a potato masher. Measure exactly 2 1/4 cups prepared strawberries into an 8 quart stockpot. Finely chop unpeeled rhubarb. Place in a saucepan. Stir in water. Bring to a boil and reduce heat and cover. Simmer for several minutes until the rhubarb is tender. Measure 1 3/4 cups prepared rhubarb into the sauce-pot with the berries and mix well. Stir in the juice of one lemon. This is an important step because pectin needs acid to set correctly.

2 Mix sugar into prepared fruit mixture. Add butter and stir. Bring to a full boil on high heat, stirring constantly until sugar dissolves. Stir in pectin. Return to a full boil and boil for 1 minute only, stirring constantly. Longer cook time begins to break down pectin. (check package directions) Remove from heat and skim off any foam.

3 Ladle at once into prepared jars, filling to within 1/8 inch of tops. Wipe jar rims and threads. Cover with 2 piece lids. Screw bands tightly. Place jars on elevated rack in canner. Lower rack into canner. Water must cover jars by 1 to 2 inches. Add boiling water, if needed. Cover and bring water to a gentle boil. Process 10 minutes, Remove jars and place upright on a towel to cool. Check seals by pressing middle of lid with finger. If lid springs back, lid is not sealed and refrigeration is necessary. **Be sure to date your jars!**

SIMPLY SUMMER PEACH PIE
SERVES: 5

Below the Mason-Dixon Line we sure love our comfort food. We take our pie as seriously as we take our sweet tea, and we'll take it anytime, anywhere – but it must be homemade. Summertime is the season to slow down the pace and revel in the simple joys that bring us so much pleasure–fresh produce from a roadside stand, glistening berries straight from the vine and precious time to spend with loved ones. You can bet your barbecue that if you drive through South Carolina on an August afternoon, you'll end up stopping at McLeod's for some sweet Georgia Belles.

Peaches, oil on canvas by Kim English.

INGREDIENTS
2 cups all-purpose flour
1 cup Crisco shortening
1/4 teaspoon salt
5 tablespoons cold water

FILLING
1 1/4 cups sugar
1 package (8 ounces) cream cheese, *at room temperature*
3/4 cup orange juice
6 1/2 cups peaches, *peeled and sliced*
1/4 cup cornstarch
1/4 cup fresh lemon juice
dash of Peach Liqueur(optional)

1. To prepare crust, combine the flour, Crisco and salt with a pastry blender. Add 5 tablespoons cold water, blend well. Roll dough mixture out onto a floured surface and spread dough evenly over pie pan. Pierce the side and bottom of crust with a fork and bake crust at 375° until golden brown, abut 20 minutes. Let crust cool on a rack.

2. FILLING. Mix cream cheese and 1/2 cup sugar until smooth. Spread cream cheese mixture evenly over bottom of cooled pastry.

3. In a food processor, blend 1 cup sliced peaches, remaining 3/4 cup sugar, orange juice and cornstarch until smooth. Pour into a 3 to 4 quart saucepan. Stir over medium heat until mixture boils and thickens, about 4 minutes. Remove from heat and stir in lemon juice and a dash of peach liqueur.

4. Add remaining 5 1/2 cups peaches to hot peach glaze and mix to coat slices. Let it cool about 25 minutes, then pour pie filling over cream cheese mixture.

5. Chill uncovered, until firm enough to cut, at least 3 hours, then serve.

Opposite Page: Peaches & Grapes, oil on canvas by Russell Gordon.

RASPBERRY CRUMP PIE WITH HOMEMADE PIE DOUGH
SERVES: 5

Read the ingredients on a store bought pie shell and you will never eat one again. Quick and simple to make your own when you place the dough between two sheets of plastic wrap. The dough doesn't stick to the counter or the rolling pin, making it so easy there's no excuse.

1. Preheat the oven to 375°. Place flour and sugar in a food processor. Pulse. Add half of the butter and pulse. Add the rest of the butter and pulse until the mixture turns into coarse crumbs.

2. Slowly add ice water through the feed tube until the dough gathers up into a ball. It may need a few more drops. Spray a little Pam on the pie plate.

3. Take the dough and flatten it into a disc and place it on a sheet of floured plastic wrap and refrigerate for 30 minutes. Then roll it out between two sheets of plastic wrap and transfer by rolling dough around the rolling pin, and transferring it to the pie plate and unroll. Gently press dough down. Prick the bottom with a fork. Line with foil and place a layer of dried beans on the foil. Bake for 15 minutes. Take it out of the oven, remove beans and foil and place it back into the oven for another 15 minutes.

4. Combine filling in a large bowl. Fill the pie plate and crumble the topping over the top. Place a pie ring shield or foil over crust to prevent over-browning. Place pie on a baking sheet and return to oven for about 1 hour. Allow to cool before serving.

INGREDIENTS
1 3/4 cup flour
1 teaspoon sugar
1 1/2 sticks butter, *cut into slices*
1/4 cup ice water

FILLING
4 (6 ounce) containers of raspberries
2 (6 ounce) containers of blackberries
1/2 cup cornstarch
1 cup sugar
1/2 teaspoon nutmeg
zest of one lemon

CRUMB TOPPING
1/2 cup flour
1/4 cup brown sugar
1/4 cup granulated sugar
1/2 cup butter, *cut into slices*
1/2 cup rolled oats
Gently toss together

SAVANNAH GREEN TOMATO COBBLER

SERVES: 6-8

Inspired by Chef Darin Sehnert of Savannah.

INGREDIENTS

1/2 cup golden raisins
1/4 cup water
1/2 cup butter
2 tablespoons dark brown sugar
1 tablespoon cornstarch
1/2 teaspoon Kosher salt
1/2 teaspoon ground nutmeg
6 green tomatoes, *cored, cut into 1/2 inch chunks*
1 tablespoon finely grated fresh ginger
1 cup sugar
1 cup self-rising flour
1 cup chopped pecans, *toasted*
1 teaspoon ground cinnamon
1 cup buttermilk

1. Preheat oven to 350°. Combine raisins and water in a microwave-safe dish. Cook for 1 minute on high. Remove from microwave and set aside while the raisins plump and cool.

2. Place butter in a 2-3 quart casserole or baking dish. Place baking dish in the oven and heat until butter is melted. While butter is melting, combine the brown sugar, cornstarch, salt, and nutmeg in a small dish and mix to combine evenly. Place diced tomatoes in a large mixing bowl and add the grated fresh ginger. Pour sugar and cornstarch mixture over the diced tomatoes and add the plumped raisins. Stir to mix well. Pour over melted butter in casserole dish.

3. In a large bowl combine the sugar, flour, toasted pecans and cinnamon. Make a well in the center of dry ingredients and pour the buttermilk into the middle. Gently fold the dry ingredients with the buttermilk until mixture is evenly moistened. Pour over the top of the tomato mixture and bake for approximately 1 hour. Serve warm.

Summer means our Lowcountry gators are out of hibernation. These majestic dinosaurs inhabit our waters & are to be respected from a safe distance.

Gator, oil on canvas by William Means Rhett, Jr.

GRAND FINALES

Our salt misted shores inspire hearty appetites and unrelenting cravings for carbohydrates. What could be better than bringing you this collection of sweets still sizzling hot from the oven. Each carefully hand formed crust is filled with little nooks and crannies containing the most decadent temptations.

CHOCOLATE FRUIT TART
SERVES: 5

Summertime is my most indulgent time of the year. Certainly excesses are enjoyed at Thanksgiving and Christmas but it's the scorch of summer that brings on the delights I most adore; blueberry tarts, strawberry-rhubarb crisp, and bowls piled high with fresh peaches and crème fraîche.

1 ALMOND PASTRY CRUST, In a food processor, pulse and finely grind the almonds. Add the flour, sugar and salt and process to blend. Add the butter and pulse until the mixture resembles coarse crumbs. With the machine running, add the egg yolk and almond extract through the feed tube and process. Add the ice water and pulse just until a dough forms. Remove from the machine. Place the dough into a 9-inch tart pan with a removable bottom, pressing the dough along the sides and then evenly across the bottom. Place in the freezer for 1/2 hour. Preheat oven to 375°

2 Line the dough with parchment paper and pie weights or beans and bake 15 minutes. Remove parchment and weights and bake until golden brown, about 10 more minutes. Allow it to cool before filling.

3 FILLING, Take out a medium bowl and combine cream cheese, confectioners' sugar, sour cream, and pudding mix. Add cream and milk beating at medium speed with an electric mixer until smooth. Spoon cream cheese mixture into the prepared crust. Cover and refrigerate for 1 hour. When ready to serve, top with strawberries, kiwis and blueberries. Brush with the melted apricot preserves. Garnish with fresh mint sprigs.

INGREDIENTS
1 (8 ounce) package cream cheese, *softened*
1/2 cup confectioners' sugar
1/3 cup sour cream
1 (3.3 ounce) box chocolate flavored instant pudding and pie mix
1 cup heavy whipping cream
1/4 cup whole milk
4 kiwis, peeled and sliced into quarters
1 pound fresh strawberries, *hulled and halved*
1/2 pint blueberries
2 tablespoons apricot preserves, *melted*
Mint sprigs for garnish (optional)

ALMOND PASTRY CRUST
1/4 cup slivered, blanched almonds, *lightly toasted and cooled*
1 1/4 cups all-purpose flour
3 tablespoons sugar
1/8 teaspoon salt
6 tablespoons, cold unsalted butter, *cut into pieces*
1 large egg yolk
1/4 teaspoon almond extract
3 tablespoons ice water

FLOURLESS CHOCOLATE CAKE WITH GANACHE
SERVES: 5

INGREDIENTS
1 cup water
3/4 cup sugar
9 tablespoons unsalted butter, *diced*
18 ounces semisweet chocolate, *chopped*
6 large eggs

Whipped Cream
1/2 cup heavy cream
1/2 teaspoon pure vanilla extract
1 teaspoon confectioners' sugar

Ganache
1 cup heavy whipping cream
8 ounces semisweet chocolate, *chopped*
dollops of lightly sweetened whipped cream

1. Preheat oven to 350°. Butter a 10-inch diameter spring-form pan. Line bottom of pan with a parchment round. Butter parchment. Wrap 3 layers of heavy-duty foil around outside of pan, bringing foil to top of rim. Combine 1 cup water and sugar in a small saucepan. Bring to a boil over medium heat, stirring until the sugar dissolves. Simmer for 5 minutes and remove from heat.

2. Melt butter in a large saucepan over low heat. Add chocolate and whisk until smooth. Whisk sugar syrup into chocolate and cool slightly. Add eggs to chocolate mixture and whisk until well blended. Pour batter into prepared pan. Place cake pan in large roasting pan. Add enough hot water to roasting pan to come halfway up sides of cake pan.

3. Bake cake until center no longer moves when pan is gently shaken, about 50 minutes. Remove from water bath and transfer to a rack. Cool completely in pan.

4. WHIPPED CREAM, In a large bowl, whip cream until stiff peaks are about to form. Beat in vanilla and sugar until peaks form. Make sure not to over-beat because the cream will then become lumpy and butter-like.

5. GANACHE, Bring whipping cream to a simmer in a small saucepan over medium heat. Remove from heat. Add chocolate and whisk until smooth. Pour over top of cake still in pan. Gently shake the pan to distribute ganache evenly over top of cake. Refrigerate cake in pan until ganache is set, about 2 hours. To release side, run knife around pan to loosen it.

PUMPKIN SPICE ICE CREAM PIE
SERVES: 10

Inspired by Chef Pat Alford, South Carolina Yacht Club.

While visiting Leopold's Ice Cream Shop on Broughton Street in Savannah, one of the city's most famous–not to mention, delicious institutions, I discovered pumpkin spice ice cream, truly decadent.

We stopped in after an adventuresome walk through Savannah's picturesque squares. Once temperatures finally dip in the fall, I love wandering around Savannah just for the pleasure of doing so without melting. The city has often been called "The Hollywood of the South," and with good reason. Surely it's a film maker's dream-come-true with all the architecturally-magnificent gems and Hollywood back-lot type places like the Mercer House, the mansion seen in *Midnight in the Garden of Good and Evil*. Another movie location in town that gets a lot of attention is Chippewa Square, where the famous park bench scene in the Tom Hanks film *Forrest Gump* was shot. In need of a break from perusing, we stopped in at Leopold's.

When he's not producing major Hollywood movies, Stratton Leopold is scooping creamy, delicious ice cream at his family's historic, old-fashion ice cream store. Leopold's prodigious film credits include *Mission: Impossible III*, and the re-make of *The Wolfman*, but he always has loved the ice cream business. In his younger years, he worked as a soda jerk in the store his Greek immigrant parents and uncles opened at Gwinnett and Habersham streets in 1919, which he and his wife, Mary, now run at their location on Broughton Street.

As we stepped inside the store, immediately we were transported back to the 1930s and 40s. From the vintage Coca-Cola logo to the white paper caps worn by soda jerks, it all takes you back to the days when famous lyricist Johnny Mercer would spend time in the store on visits to Savannah.

INGREDIENTS
2 pints (or 1/2 gallon) pure vanilla ice cream
1 cup canned pumpkin
1/2 cup packed brown sugar
1 teaspoon ground ginger
1/2 teaspoon ground cinnamon
1/2 teaspoon ground nutmeg
1 tablespoon orange juice
1/4 cup Hershey's chocolate syrup drizzled

CRUST
1 1/2 cups gingersnap crumbs
2 tablespoons sugar
1/2 teaspoon pure vanilla extract
1/4 cup butter, melted

1. Preheat the oven to 350°. Process gingersnap cookies in food processor until crumbled or simply put the cookies into a Ziploc bag and crush with a rolling pin.

2. Mix the crumbs with the sugar, vanilla and butter until combined.

3. Press mixture firmly and evenly against the bottom and side of a 9 inch pie pan. Bake 10 minutes. Set aside to cool.

4. FILLING, 2 pints Pumpkin Spice Ice Cream

5. CRUST, use a large bowl and combine the softened ice cream, pumpkin, brown sugar, ginger, cinnamon, nutmeg and orange juice and pour into the crust.

6. When the crust is cool, remove ice cream from freezer. Allow to soften. When soft, spread both pints of ice cream over the bottom of the crust. Cover with foil and freeze until very hard. Drizzle with Hershey's chocolate syrup. To serve, cut slices of pie on individual plates and enjoy a little slice of heaven on a plate!

CAROLINA GOLD RICE PUDDING
SERVES: 4

Inspired by Chef Tom Ferrell of Berkeley Hall.

Egg Beater, oil on linen by Hilarie Lambert.

INGREDIENTS

3 tablespoons unsalted butter
1 quart whole milk
1 cup Carolina Gold rice
1 vanilla bean, split or *1 teaspoon pure vanilla extract*
1/3 cup golden raisins
1 cup sugar
1 teaspoon cinnamon
1 cup chopped sugared pecans

1. SUGARED PECANS, Toss in a small amount of water, just to moisten. Toss in granulated sugar to coat. Bake in 350° oven for 5 - 10 minutes.

2. In a heavy duty stockpot heat milk with butter and vanilla to the point of boiling. Add rice at this point while stirring with a wooden spoon.

3. Continue to cook the rice according to package directions, stirring to prevent rice from sticking to the bottom of the pot.

4. The starch from the rice will thicken the milk after about 30 minutes. When this occurs, add raisins, sugar and cinnamon. Simmer an additional 5-10 minutes.

5. Turn off the heat once thickened but not thick enough to where the spoon will stand up. Remove vanilla bean, if using. Sprinkle with sugared pecans.

EDNA LEWIS' FRESH APPLE CAKE

SERVES: 10

Edna Lewis, Former Chef at Middleton Place in Charleston

This lovely cake has some real gravitas. In Charleston, teatime was observed for the purpose of tasting great rare, rich, and mostly sweet Madeira estate wines from the islands ruled by Portugal. It wasn't unusual for "Tea" to last at least an hour and maybe two, every day. From today's perspective, it's difficult to imagine a society with the idle time to indulge in "tea" on a daily basis.

1. Preheat oven to 325°; Put sugars and oil in a mixing bowl and beat until well blended. Add the eggs one at a time, beating well after each addition

2. Sift together the flour, cinnamon, baking soda, nutmeg and salt. Gradually add the flour mixture to the wet ingredients, mixing just until well blended. Stir in the vanilla, pecans, and apples and pour onto a greased and floured 9 x 13 pan.

3. Bake until a toothpick inserted into the center of the cake comes out clean, about 1 1/4 hours, beginning to check after 50 minutes. Remove from oven and let cool while preparing glaze.

INGREDIENTS

1 cup light brown sugar, packed
1 cup sugar
1 1/2 cups vegetable oil
3 eggs
3 cups all-purpose flour
1 teaspoon baking soda
2 teaspoons cinnamon
1/2 teaspoon nutmeg
1/2 teaspoon salt
5 Granny Smith apples, *diced into 1/2 inch pieces*
1 1/4 cup chopped pecans
2 1/4 teaspoons pure vanilla extract

GLAZE

4 tablespoons unsalted butter
1/4 cup sugar
1/4 cup light brown sugar
 pinch of salt
1/2 cup heavy cream
Stir together

SAVANNAH, GEORGIA

Picturesque squares, moss-draped live oaks and molasses-sweet charm, Savannah, like Charleston and other Southern port cities, is forever linked to its past. Established in 1733, this historic city may be enjoyed on a carriage ride where guides will lead you down cobblestone streets to visit places of long ago. Linger awhile among the magnolias and dogwoods and soak in the ambiance of this truly magnificent city.

Market Street Savannah, oil on canvas by Walt Gonske.

FRESH STRAWBERRIES OVER CORN FLAKE RUSK

SERVES: 4

Inspired by Chef Tom Ferrell of Berkeley Hall.

We Southerners are famous for having a sweet tooth as evidenced by the amount of sugar we put in our sweet tea. But the craving is about more than just a special affinity for all things sugared. Many times the foods we crave and dream about are attached to childhoods memories of friends and family. It's not so much about the food itself, it's the emotional experience bonding us to it forever.

Southerners use sweets to indulge personal nostalgia, demonstrate gracious hospitality, and mark special occasions. Although I'm more of a cook than a baker, I find myself with an endless collection of pies, tarts, cobblers, cookies and custards. The sweets of my childhood have found their way into my kitchen from the generations of women in my family, my mother, my aunts and grandmothers and for that I am thankful.

The desserts featured in this chapter will encourage friends and family to linger awhile longer around your southern table. Great food and friends just go together.

1. Cut out center of bread slices. Combine eggs, milk and vanilla extract. Dip each slice of bread in egg, then crushed corn flakes. When ready to eat, lightly deep fry until golden brown.

2. SYRUP, Place sugar and cider in a small sauce pan reducing to half. Add Grand Marnier and simmer for a few more minutes and allow to cool.

3. CREAM, In a cold stainless steel mixing bowl, whisk cream with orange zest until stiff peaks start to form. Then fold in sugar and continue to whisk until peaks form.

4. Layer strawberry slices with points facing outward over Rusk. Place a dollop of citrus cream on top and drizzle with balsamic reduction and cider syrup.

INGREDIENTS
4 slices Texas toast, *cut with a 3 inch round cutter*
1 quart crushed corn flakes
2 eggs
1/2 cup milk
1 teaspoon pure vanilla extract
1 quart large strawberries, *sliced*

CIDER SYRUP
1/2 cup sugar
1/2 cup apple cider
1 tablespoon Grand Marnier

BALSAMIC REDUCTION
3/4 cup balsamic vinegar
Reduce over low heat to 1/3 the amount and allow to cool.

CREAM
1 cup heavy whipping cream
1 tablespoon powdered sugar
zest of 1 orange, *reserve a small amount for garnish*

INDEX

A

ALMOND PASTRY CRUST, 130

AMBROSE FARMS, 35

AMEN STREET FISH & RAW BAR, 99

AMEN STREET SHRIMP & GRITS, 99

ANSON MILLS, 49

ANTOINE'S RESTAURANT, 22

ARUGULA PESTO, 33

B

BALSAMIC REDUCTION, 138

BASIC CHICKEN STOCK, 102

BERKELEY HALL, 94, 134, 138

BERNIE MALEY, 86

BETTY ANGLIN SMITH, 25, 117, 142

BILLY'S VENISON MEDALLIONS, 65

BISCUIT, 18

BISQUE OF WINTER SQUASH, 111

BLACKENED MAHI ON TOMATO COULIS, 98

BLACKENED SEASONING, 98

BLUE CHEESE SAUCE, 77

BLUE CRAB, 86

BLUFFTON, 45

BLUFFTON OYSTER FACTORY, 20

BRAISED SHORT RIBS ON POLENTA, 76

BROWN RICE MUFFINS, 59

C

CAPRESE APPETIZER, 26

CAROLINA CORN PUDDING, 41

CAROLINA GOLD RICE, 74

CAROLINA GOLD RICE PUDDING, 134

CAROL PEEK, 74, 143

CASHEW BROWN RICE SALAD, 57

CHARLESTON GOLD RICE, 58

CHARLESTON SHRIMP PILAU, 58

CHARLES WARREN MUNDY, 143

CHARLIE STERNBURGH, 45

CHEF BRANDON BUCK, 70

CHEF DARIN SEHNERT, 19, 127

CHEF KEVIN CAVANAUGH, 16, 17, 105

CHEF PAT ALFORD, 132

CHEF RAMON TAIMANGLO, 99

CHEF ROBERT WYSONG, 36, 39, 53, 92

CHEF SEAN BROCK, 95

CHEF SHERRI WHITMIRE, 35

CHEF TOM FERRELL, 94, 134, 138

CHEF TREY DUTTON, 114

CHICKEN & WATERMELON SALAD, 120

CHOCOLATE FRUIT TART, 130

CIDER SYRUP, 138

COLLETON RIVER PLANTATION, 53, 92

COLLETON RIVER PLANTATION., 36

CRAB & BEAN SALAD, 88

CRAB & CORN FRITTERS, 17

CRANBERRY MAPLE SAUCE, 78

CRAZY CRAB BENEDICT, 95

CREAMY WASABI DRESSING, 85

CRUMB TOPPING, 126

CRUST, 132

C.W. MUNDY, 109

D

DAN MCCAW, 26, 142

DAVID HETTINGER, 30, 142

DOVES WITH BACON CREAM SAUCE, 66

E

EDNA LEWIS, 135

EDNA LEWIS' FRESH APPLE CAKE, 135

ELIZABETH POLLIE, 143

F

FABULOUS BAKED GRITS, 56

FIRE ROASTED COCKTAIL SAUCE, 16

FLOURLESS CHOCOLATE CAKE WITH GANACHE, 131

FRENCH CHICKEN IN WHITE WINE SAUCE, 74

FRESH STRAWBERRIES OVER CORN FLAKE RUSK, 138

FRIED GREEN TOMATO BLT PO BOYS, 45

FRITTER BATTER, 17

FROGMORE STEW ON A STICK, 16

G

GANACHE, 131

GARDENS CORNER MOTEL AND RESTAURANT, 44

GEECHIE BOY CREAMY GRITS, 54

GEECHIE BOY MARKET AND MILL, 54

GLAZE, 135

GLENN ROBERTS, 49

GRAINGER MCCOY, 65

GRANDPAPPY'S POKE SALLET, 32

GRITS, 99

H

HAM & PIMENTO CHEESE PARTY BISCUITS, 18

HEIRLOOM GRAINS & GOLDEN FRUIT SALAD, 53

HERITAGE GOLF TOURNAMENT, 15

HILARIE LAMBERT, 6, 40, 56, 59, 118, 142

HILTON HEAD ISLAND, 16

HOLIDAY CHICKEN SALAD, 75

HOLLANDAISE SAUCE, 95

HUDSON'S SEAFOOD HOUSE ON THE DOCKS, 98

I

ICED PINEAPPLE MINT TEA, 19

J

JAMBALAYA STRUDEL, 94

JAMES BEARD, 105

JEFF NEALE, 68

JEKYLL ISLAND, 86

JENNIFER SMITH ROGERS, 11, 25, 99, 104

JIM PALMER, 16, 143

JOE BOWLER, 10, 43

JOHN CARROLL DOYLE, 34, 44, 49, 53, 54, 142

JOHN EGERTON, 120

JOHN ENCINIAS, 111, 143

JOHNNY CAKES, 71

JOHNSON & WALES, 39

JOSEPH ORR, 22, 143

K

KATHLEEN DUNPHY, 30, 142

KATHY CROWTHER, 18, 142

KIM ENGLISH, 33, 125, 142

L

LAURIE MEYER, 79, 143

LEOPOLD'S ICE CREAM SHOP, 132

LIME VINAIGRETTE DRESSING, 120

LORAN SPECK, 120, 143

M

MAMA'S BUTTER BEAN & CORN SUCCOTASH, 40
MARILYN SIMANDLE, 57, 114
MARK HORTON, 58, 88, 107, 142
MAY RIVER GRILL, 45
MICHAEL B. KARAS, 77, 103, 142
MICHAEL HARRELL, 83, 90, 107, 142
MIDDLETON BAKED GUINEA HEN, 70
MIDDLETON PLACE PLANTATION, 68, 135
MIDDLETON PLACE PORK BELLY & JOHNNY CAKES, 71
MILDRED HUIE WILCOX, 108
MILDRED NIX HUIE, 108
MUSHROOM POLENTA STUFFED COLLARD GREENS, 35
MUSSELS MARINIERE, 91
MUSTARD WINE SAUCE, 94

N

NANCY HOERTER, 32
NANCY RICKER RHETT, 3, 4, 17, 44, 45, 70, 119, 143

O

OYSTERS BIENVILLE, 22
OYSTERS ROCKEFELLER, 20

P

PALMETTO BLUFF, 114
PAN-FRIED QUAIL & COUNTRY GRAVY, 64
PARMIGIANO-REGGIANO SAUCE, 56
PARSLEY OIL, 36
PAT CONROY, 62, 96
PEACH GINGER JAM, 119
PECAN CRUSTED PORK TENDERLOIN, 78
PEPPERCORN CRUSTED BEEF TENDERLOIN, 77
PEPPER VINEGAR, 32
PETER ROLFE, 70, 96, 143
PLANTATION PICKLED OKRA, 117
POACHED EGGS, 95
PRINCE OF TIDES, 62
PUMPKIN SPICE ICE CREAM PIE, 132

R

RASPBERRY CRUMP PIE WITH HOMEMADE PIE DOUGH, 126
REMOULADE SAUCE, 45, 92
RHETT THURMAN, 102, 143
ROASTED RED PEPPER SAUCE, 41
ROASTED TOMATO PUREE, 99
RON VIDO, 69
RUSSELL GORDON, 83, 125
RUSTIC HEIRLOOM TOMATO SALAD, 121

S

SAVANNAH GREEN TOMATO COBBLER, 127
SEAFOOD SPICE, 92
SEA ISLAND SHRIMP BISQUE, 103
SEARED AHI TUNA SALAD, 85
SERIOUS SOUTHERN STROGANOFF, 79
SHANNON RUNQUIST, 83, 143
SHANNON SMITH HUGHES, 25, 39, 49, 142
SHE CRAB SOUP, 105
SHERRY VINAIGRETTE, 88
SHRIMP, CRAB & BEAN SALAD, 88
SIMPLY SUMMER PEACH PIE, 125
SOFT SHELL CRAB, 92
SOUTH CAROLINA YACHT CLUB, 16, 17, 105, 132
SOUTHERN BUTTERMILK CORNBREAD, 50
ST. HELENA ISLAND, 16, 35
STRAWBERRY - RHUBARB JAM, 122
STRAWBERRY SALAD, 25
ST. SIMONS CRAB STEW, 108
SUGARED PECANS, 134
SUNBURY CRAB COMPANY, 86
SWEET CORN CHOW-CHOW, 114
SWEET POTATO BUTTER, 118

T

TED ELLIS, 121, 142
TOMATO PUREE, 99
TOMATO SAUCE, 35
TONY GRAY, 20

V

VIC'S, 102
VIC'S FRENCH ONION SOUP, 102
VINAIGRETTE, 25

W

WALTER GREER, 84, 142
WALT GONSKE, 19, 42, 137, 142
WILLIAM MEANS RHETT, JR., 62, 64, 65, 66, 127, 143
WILLIAM RHETT III, 49, 143
WINTER SQUASH, 111

Z

ZIP'S SWEET POTATO SOUFFLÉ, 44

THE ARTISTS

Kathy Crowther

Kathy's creative formula combines her love of nature and its exacting details with a fascination for geometric designs. Her trademark is borders where she paints over the framing mat, lending a sense of continual growth and profusion of color.

John Carroll Doyle

American Impressionist whose artwork depicts the Lowcountry life around Charleston, S.C. with passion and understanding. He is nationally known for his energetic, light filled paintings of subjects as diverse as blues musicians, to blue marlins.

Kathleen Dunphy

Certain to be among the next generation of great plein air painters. She is one of those rare people who have true passion, dedication, and a gift for transposing nature's beauty to the canvas.

Ted Ellis

"I'm on a personal journey to pictorially document our life history through painting and share that experience with the world... that is my passion." Ellis has been a champion in the establishment of African American art as a national treasure.

John Encinias

He is a longtime member of the National Academy of Western Art and is largely self taught. He is equally adept at still lifes and landscapes. For his landscapes, he is a "plein aire painter, completing his canvases outside.

Kim English

Depicts in his paintings the simple beauty found in daily life. All of his paintings are completed in one sitting because he believes immediacy is important. Not only because it is often the nature of people, but for him it is the most instinctive way to paint.

Walter Greer

Closely associated in his oil painting with Hilton Head Island, Walter Greer is the first artist to have made the island his permanent residence. He has lived on the island since 1960 and spends much of his time in the woods, beaches, and marshes which he depicts in his signature "pond series."

Walt Gonske

"My goal in the work is not to show what I know, but what I feel. The more intensely I can express emotion through paint about the subject, the more likely the viewer will respond."

Michael Harrell

He is rarely far from water where he depicts real people in real environments close to the ocean's edge with a depth of perception well beyond his years.

David Hettinger

He is a Master Signature Member of the Oil Painters of America. He has won both regional and national awards for works that continue to strike a resonant chord with collectors who have snapped up his paintings for more than 30 years.

Mark Horton

Horton is particularly fascinated with the effects of light and weather upon the landscape. He paints beyond a literal interpretation of a scene to portray nature in a way that reflects his own ideas and sensibilities while capturing the spirit, color and changing light of a place.

Shannon Smith Hughes

Daughter of renowned painter Betty Anglin Smith of Charleston. Her varied subject matter is united by her emphasis on light. Her eye is looking and constantly aware and in tune with the light, painting whatever strikes her.

Michael B. Karas

Karas is recognized by collectors and fellow artists as one of the nation's finest marine and landscape painters. The extraordinary oil paintings created by Michael B. Karas, evolve with passion and self-imposed standards of excellence, making them internationally prized and treasured.

Hilarie Lambert

She enjoys painting the familiar, revealing the beauty in what we might have forgotten or gotten too busy to notice – the magic of everyday life. Although Lambert has won numerous awards, what keeps her painting is not the life outside the studio, but the life inside it.

Laurie Meyer

She has lived and painted in Charleston, S.C. for over 25 years. Following careers in education and corporate sales, Laurie is now devoting her life to her first love – painting.

She paints with rich color and broad "brushy" strokes and palette knife to express the unique and recognizable softness in her work.

Dan McCaw

He is an artist with a single vision: to create the most expressive visual experience possible based upon a wide variety of personal observations. "Good paintings are like friends," he has said, "they encourage you to do more, to search, to experiment and to grow."

Charles Warren Mundy

A world-renowned American Impressionist who believes, "the power of the suggestive is much greater than the statement of reality." This true renaissance man is a member of the Disco Mountain Boys, a popular Indy-based bluegrass band of other highly-skilled musicians committed to their current professions, yet in need of a musical outlet.

Joseph Orr

He paints landscapes capturing the essence and tranquility of the scene. Using light and shadow to convey mood and flavor of an ethereal moment, his paintings are works of art centered on scenes of solitude.

Jim Palmer

One of the first artists to make a permanent residence on Hilton Head Island, he specializes in Lowcountry scenes that now grace homes and businesses throughout the country.

Carol Peek

Her work has been shown in galleries and museums from San Francisco to New York City for over 25 years. Peek's work has won numerous awards and she currently is represented by The North Point Gallery in San Francisco, CA. Calabi Gallery, Petaluma, CA, and Morris and Whiteside Gallery, Hilton Head.

Elizabeth Pollie

Harboring a deep love of travel and art history, Elizabeth has combined her travels with her painting practice. The images she creates are imbued with a sense of poetry, mood and depth. She is the recipient of numerous awards and her work s celebrated both here and abroad.

Nancy Ricker Rhett

She is an original in every sense of the word. Completely true to herself, she is a self-taught artist, historian, world traveler and consummate Southern lady. She is equally at home with a shotgun in hand hunting quail, or in her home studio painting Lowcountry scenes, birds, trees, flowers and indigenous birds.

William Means Rhett, Jr & William Rhett III

Represent five generations of artists and many important family connections. Nancy Rhett's relatives, who have been in Beaufort since the late 1600s as land grant colonists, have names such as Elliott, Heyward and Pinckney. Both Rhetts are descended from talented artists and interestingly, none of the talented Rhetts have had any formal artistic training.

Peter Rolfe

Rolfe is a self-taught artist who paints primarily in oil, but also uses watercolor, gouache, acrylic and pastels. Formally he worked for Westinghouse until the late 1970s when he began to dabble in painting.

Shannon Runquist

Shannon is a Realist Painter born in Savannah, Georgia who has spent most of her life in the coastal and rural South. She finds inspiration in the Lowcountry of South Carolina and the elements and history that define it.

Betty Anglin Smith

Betty is a native of the Carolinas and firmly established in Charleston's art community. With a style consisting of large brush strokes and bold, vibrant colors, Smith is noted for her expansive marsh vistas, beaches and waterways.

Loran Speck "1943 - 2011"

He was a self-described "natural realist," who believes his work reflects his personality, including his simplicity and love of quiet intimacy. Loran was known for his masterful talent, but also for being a humble and gracious and truly kind man. (Copyright Loran Speck Living Trust)

Rhett Thurman

Rhett has been painting in Charleston for over 40 years and 25 years teaching studio art at the Gibbes Museum. This artist needs no one's permission to manipulate her unconventional palette of warm, unblended colors into luminous signature scenes. You might say that Thurman and the Charleston art community have grown up together.

Marilyn Simandle

Marilyn is a master Signature Member of Oil Painters of America (OPA), a Signature member of the American Watercolor Society, Plein-Air Painters of America (PAPA) and the California Art Club.

RESOURCES

ANSON MILLLS

THE STAFF AT MIDDLETON PLACE

THE STAFF AT BERKELEY HALL

PALMETTO BLUFF PLANTATION

THE STAFF AT COLLETON RIVER

HUDSONS SEAFOOD ON THE DOCKS

THE SOUTH CAROLINA YACHT CLUB

AMEN CORNER FISH AND RAW BAR

VIC'S SAVANNAH

GARDEN AND GUN MAGAZINE

THE LOCAL PALATE

CHARLESTON MAGAZINE

THE SOUTH MAGAZINE

SAVANNAH MAGAZINE

POST AND COURIER.COM

THE NEW YORK TIMES

SAVANNAH DAILY NEWS

MILDRED HUIE WILCOX OF ST. SIMONS

LINDSAY GIFFORD OF PINK MAGAZINE

LOWCOUNTRY COOKING JOHN MARTIN TAYLOR

SPORTING CLASSICS MAGAZINE

NANCY AND WILLIAM MEANS RHETT, JR.

LEIGH LIMEHOUSE - SMITH KILLIAN FINE ART

JOHN CARROLL DOYLE GALLERY

HORTON HAYES GALLERY, CHARLESTON

THE HISTORIC CHARLESTON FOUNDATION

MORRIS - WHITESIDE GALLERY

GAY SEAFOOD COMPANY

BLUFFTON OYSTER HOUSE

SUNBURY CRAB COMPANY

AMBROSE FARMS

FRANK STITT'S "BOTTEGA FAVORITA"